D0734405

Doing

What

Is

Christian

Doing
What
Is
Christian

Harold A. Bosley

HENRY M. BULLOCK, *General Editor*

GRADED PRESS
NASHVILLE, TENNESSEE

DOING WHAT IS CHRISTIAN

Copyright, 1960 by Graded Press

Graded Press

201 Eighth Avenue, South, Nashville 3, Tennessee

To Mr. and Mrs. J. M. Willson
Donors of the Willson Lectureships in many colleges.
On whose generosity many depend.
On whose Christian friendship, I rely.

ACKNOWLEDGMENTS

Portions of chapters 1, 3, 4, 7, 8, and 9 develop further lines of thought that I originally introduced in the following books: *A Firm Faith for Today,* 1950, Harper and Brothers; *Preaching On Controversial Issues,* 1953, Harper and Brothers; *Main Issues Confronting Protestantism,* 1948, Harper and Brothers; and *What Did The World Council Say To You?* 1955, Abingdon Press.

HAROLD A. BOSLEY

FOREWORD

THE TITLE Basic Christian Books aptly describes the character of the twelve volumes which comprise this series. They are basic; they are Christian; they are books.

The studies are basic in that they deal with the areas in which all adults should be informed in order to be thoughtful members of their religious communities. These include (1) The Faith, (2) The Church, (3) The Christian Life, and (4) The World.

Again, the studies are Christian since they are written in the light of the meaning of the gospel of Jesus Christ, with its many facets which extend into all of life. Personal religious experience, the home, other religions, church membership, missions, the Scriptures, doctrine, Christian action, the ecumenical movement, church history, Methodist heritage, evangelism, and Christian education—each of these is considered and thoughtfully interpreted from the Christian viewpoint, book by book.

The series is written for lay persons and in non-technical language, although the authorship is highly distinguished in the several fields in which the authors write. The treatment of the subjects is brief, but it is never shallow. The books, more or less, have the character of a primer that emphasizes essentials in bold outline with a minimum of detail.

The Basic Christian Books may be fitted into the program of adults in a variety of ways. Many will wish to use them as an elective course in a Sunday morning class hour or in a Sunday evening fellowship session. Leadership helps in booklet form will be available for each book, so that teaching aids and group guidance will facilitate their use.

Doing What Is Christian is the fifth volume in the Basic Christian Books series. Its purpose is to bring us face to face with the call of Christ as the church bears her witness in the world. The author deals both with the gospel that is to be proclaimed and with the society in which it is to be expressed.

Throughout the centuries there have been different interpretations of the gospel on the one hand, and of the nature of the Christian witness that the church is to make on the other. This is no less true today. And even within our own denomination where The Methodist Church has officially expressed her positions in the *Discipline,* there are individual Methodists who sincerely differ with these views, and who are a vital part of our fellowship. Some would liberalize them even further; others would make them more conservative.

A study of *Doing What Is Christian* will provide an occasion for re-thinking our basic stand in regard to such questions as temperance, family life, race, economics, government, war and peace, and ecumenical relations. This is all to the good.

The author, Harold A. Bosley, has written a stimulating book. He is recognized as an incisive thinker and a prophetic preacher. Minister of the First Methodist Church, Evanston, Illinois, he is also giving vigorous leadership in the World Council of Churches.

Appreciation should be expressed to Mrs. Freddie Henry Schisler for her work in connection with the editing of the manuscript.

CHARLES M. LAYMON
Editor
Adult Publications

Contents

CHAPTER

1

God Is Love

I

THERE are two general ways of proceeding in the con-
struction of what might be called the philosophical
foundations of the Christian way of life. One begins with and
moves from the New Testament to our life. The other begins
with our own experience and uses the New Testament as
a reservoir in the development of a Christian perspective on
it. Either way is legitimate and, if carefully done, will prove
helpful. The latter is used in Part I. This section begins
with a characterization of the world in which we live, the
world of our own experience, and then seeks to relate the
meaning of essential historical Christian affirmations to it.

The base line in the Christian witness is in the great
commandment itself: "Thou shalt love the Lord thy God
with all thy heart, and with all thy soul, and with all thy
strength, and with all thy mind; and thy neighbour as thy-
self." (Luke 10:27.) Closely related to it is the conclusion
drawn by the writer of I John: "God is love."

There has never been any serious argument in the Chris-

11

tian tradition over the centrality of this conviction about the nature of God, though there has been a continuing discussion of its meaning. The Christian tradition has produced many serious and provocative interpretations of the idea of God; but none of them contravenes and all relate themselves creatively to the faith that "God is love." If we accept the idea that "God is love," this becomes for us the foundation for the Christian way of living. Let us, therefore, examine what this conviction means in the experiences of everyday living and in the understanding of human life and history.

II

Dr. Charles Hartshorne begins his exacting, logical study of the meaning of the idea of God with the simple assertion: "The ground then for this book is the conviction that a magnificent intellectual content—far surpassing that of such systems as Thomism, Spinozism, German idealism, positivism (old and new)—is implicit in the religious faith most briefly expressed in the three words, God is love." [1] As we examine at closer range this "magnificent intellectual content" we shall find it firmly based on certain large areas of important facts.

Before sketching these, we need to have clearly in mind the unusual meaning which the New Testament pours into the word "love."

The Greeks used three words for various forms of love: *eros, philia,* and *agape. Eros* "means passionate yearning after another person." *Philia* "generally indicate[s] liking or caring, as of gods for men, of friend for friend, the love that is given to all kinds of human beings, the love of Antigone

[1] Charles Hartshorne, *Man's Vision of God* (New York, Harper & Brothers, 1941), page ix. Used by permission.

when she says she was made for mutual affection." *Agape* must be regarded as a sort of "sleeper" word in terms of its usage by the Greeks. They used it very little; its development as a central idea awaited Christian thinkers. For the Greek its meaning was "colourless and indefinite." [2]

There are glints of a deeper meaning when it suggests a strong preference for another and an actual identification of one's self with the welfare of another. It indicates a very special relationship born of deep and in many cases undeserved affection. Small wonder the early Christians seized on *agape* when they wanted to find a word that would interpret their experience of the outpouring of the undeserved love of God in Jesus Christ. When Paul is writing of love in 1 Corinthians 13, he uses *agape,* and by it means a feeling of oneness, community, mutuality, togetherness, brotherhood of man with man in the spirit of God as found in Jesus Christ.

III

When we make the claim that God is love and seek to document it with facts in our time, it takes on three special meanings: one has to do with the nature of the universe in which we live; the second, with the special nature of human beings; the third, with the special nature of human society.

Love denotes the principle of order, purpose, structure or development in this universe which manifests itself on the level of human life in the growth of values and the value relationships through which life unfolds. God, so conceived, is a concrete principle or power, giving stability,

[2] *Bible Key Words,* from Gerhard Kittel's *Theologisches Worterbuch zum Neuen Testament,* translated and edited by J. R. Coates. Book I, *Love,* by Gottfried Quell and Ethelbert Stauffer. (New York, Harper & Bros., 1951), pages 25-28.

definiteness, purpose, and creativity to the universe. This "vision" of the meaning of God has stirred some of the great philosophical minds of our time much as the "vision" of the Copernican universe affected Bruno.

Some impressive systems of modern thought are efforts to explore its fuller meaning in terms of the problems it raises. For these thinkers, God is a necessary principle of interpretation of the character of the world as known. God is no projection of weak and fearful men; rather he is the literal foundation of all reality. Difficult as it is to understand God, it is literally impossible to understand or to interpret the world apart from God. He is not a mechanical structure or order; he is the source, the sustainer, and the recreator of life. Even though he is the One in whose will the stars find their way, he is also and as truly the One in whose will each human being finds his way.

To call God "the Wholly Other" is a form of metaphysical nonsense reserved for those who refuse to examine the plain as well as the possible implications of known facts about this universe. God is no more "wholly other" than life is "wholly other"; or we are "wholly other." God is more than life and infinitely more than any form of life, but he is the creative principle that underlies and never abandons life.

The notion of denying the existence or relevance of God may have been possible when he was regarded as a tribal war god, sitting on a mountaintop, and limited by race or national loyalty. But when the principle of development and purpose in the universe becomes the fact indicated by the word "God," he must be accepted as a fundamental principle of understanding and interpretation. God is the difference between a cosmos and a chaos. This, then, in brief form, is a basic fact which gives substance to the ancient declaration that "God is love."

IV

The second meaning of this assertion is to be found in terms of our own nature as human beings. The principle of development finds its expression in human life in the growth of values and the value relationships that give life its meaning. Man's very being is the result of the sharing of life with life in and through his parents. The intimate relationships of friendship and love are the environment in which life unfolds most normally. That is the deepest reason why man needs them. We cannot live alone and like it; in fact, we cannot live alone at all and be a human being. This is the way we are made by the creative power we call God. He made us, not alone for himself, but for each other.

The greatest value in life is God's hand on one's shoulder leading him toward the unfoldment of life. We live neither by bread alone nor by ourselves alone; we are bound in one "bundle of life" with all other men whether we want it or not—and the life we have demands for its completeness intimate, creative, dependable relationships with other people. Friendship and love, then, are not luxuries, but are basic necessities of life.

A person finds in his relationship to his group, whether it be social, business, or otherwise, some of the most abiding satisfactions. Indeed those relationships help him to achieve the most creative results for himself and others.

To say this is to accept the fact that these relationships which we take so for granted drive their taproot in the very heart of the universe itself. Men need one another because God in his wisdom made life that way. Friendship and love are his will for our life; his mandatory way toward the full life; his way of revealing the hidden depths of meaning in our common life.

V

The third meaning of the affirmation "God is love" refers to the nature of society and especially to the idea of brotherhood, community, or oneness. The factual content of this notion is prefigured in the social nature of man. We do not decide to be social; we are made that way, and we must live that way or perish. Rivalry, conflict, and warfare have been the bane of our existence from the beginning of time. From the Christian point of view any effort to treat them as normal and accept them accordingly has finally had to be dismissed. This is because men have dreamed of a peaceful world and they have sensed the meaning of what is right and just. Springing from the depths of our social nature is the desire for community, the yearning for a real sense of belonging to all men everywhere. Coupled with this is the vision of the day when brotherhood will prevail throughout the human family.

Out of this dream come the positive impulses which have supported the League of Nations, the World Court, and the United Nations. Fear, of itself, can no more explain the almost pathetic hope with which each such effort is greeted by mankind than it can explain the origin of religion itself. If successive failures could discourage a hope, this one would have died long ago. But the vision of world brotherhood rests on a more substantial foundation than a prudence born of any tally of successes and failures in our efforts to realize it.

It is the contention of Christian thought that God's will for human life is at once the real foundation in fact of the vision for peace and the judgment of every effort to realize that vision. God's will is also the reason why every effort to stabilize the world on any other basis is doomed to fail. It is the will of God that men who are brothers one of another should not rest until they bring into being a condition of mutuality and oneness in the human family.

VI

The belief that "God is love" is not to be taken as an act of blind or irrational faith. God is not a religious postulate, a pious hope, flung into the unknown by men standing on the edge of the known. God, as we have been describing him, is a demonstrably rational inference not so much permitted as required by the very structure of known facts. He is a personally experienced power and reality in human life and history. He is the unifying character or nature clearly discernible and experienced in reality.

This is not to say that we can either "find God" in a test tube or exhaust his meaning in a syllogism. But the order of fact found in a test tube, or stateable in terms of a syllogism, is an integral aspect of a much larger order of fact characteristic of the universe in which we live. It is therefore *a valid clue to its nature*. God not only can be, God is known: known to be a fact; known to be a distinctive kind of fact; known to be the one fundamental fact in life and history. God is known not only as an essential aspect of reality, abstractly conceived, but also as the very heart of the life process of the universe; he is known through experience as the creator and sustainer of the values which, when chosen and followed, underlie the creative relationships of life. God is known also as judge of false values which impoverish and finally destroy the very meaning of life. He is known as the One in whom we live and move and have our being.

God who is love can be loved: We love him as the one on whom we are dependent for life, and for the possibility of the good life. We love him as the Creator and Sustainer of all creative relationships with colleagues, friends and loved ones. We love him as the One in whose eternal nature and will the great and good facts of life have their final validation and ultimate strength. We love him as the One whose will for us as seen in the life and teachings of Jesus Christ is so filled with understanding, compassion, tenderness, and mercy as to require the highest and holiest word we know, even "love." We love him as the One in whom life finds its origin, meaning, and ultimate destination beyond the reach of death. As Jesus said, we are to love him "with all our heart, with all our soul, with all our mind, and with all our strength."

The God of love can and must be served by those who accept and respond to his love. Every person is to serve him— not as a slave serves a master, nor as a prisoner serves the jailer, nor a subject the tyrant. But he is to serve God as a dutiful son serves a wise and good father—with love, joy, understanding, and trust. We must serve God with our mind in order that we may be able to give a reason for the hope that is within us; with our will that we may earnestly seek to do his will for our life and time. We are to serve with our entire life, knowing that, finally, the only effective token of belief is life itself—a life made radiant by the love and the will of God.

God is to be served with an awareness of real freedom and responsibility, because he has chosen to give us the high privilege and calling of being co-workers together with him in the creation of his Kingdom in human life and history. God is to be served with singleness of mind and spirit, because every road away from or in defiance of his will is the road away from the great value relationships which give meaning to life. What is even more important, God is to be served because the roads which lead toward him lead to the most abundant life dreamed of by man.

Any attempt then to construct the meaning of the Christian witness rests on the deep conviction that God is this abiding meaningfulness of life, this essential togetherness of values; this firm purpose in the universe in terms of which life finds purpose and meaning. God, so conceived, is love and is the peace that passeth all understanding.

Augustine put it in a series of very human similes: "God is medicine to the unhealthy, rule to the crooked, light to the darkened, dwelling to the homeless."

2

Jesus Christ Is the Way

I

THE TASK of the Christian witness is the same today as always: to present Jesus Christ to our generation. He is the heart of everything that bears the name "Christian." We can have a religious organization without him, but not a Christian church—for he is the head and the heart of the church. We can have a noble religious ethic and morality without him, but not the Christian ethic and morality—for he is the incarnation of the values, motives, and driving power of these. We can live an upright personal life without him, but not a Christian life—for loyalty to him, commitment to him, and confidence in his teachings nurture the attitudes, release the energies, and set the far-flung goals that distinguish the Christian life. We can have the Old Testament without him but not the New—for he is the New Testament. It revolves around him as a wheel around an axle. He is the heart of the Christian faith and witness in this and every other day.

This fact is driven home in a most dramatic way in Charles Sheldon's famous book, *In His Steps*. The subtitle— indeed, the question around which the book revolves—is "What would Jesus do?" The purpose of the book is to present Jesus Christ as a contemporary and to measure the difference he would make in our common life. While the book is far from profound, it continues to catch and hold the interest of thousands of readers. It has struck so responsive a chord in the human heart that it has sold more copies than all other novels of religious background taken together. Second only to the Bible as a best seller, it has appeared in almost every language known to man, and its appeal is far from dead.

The explanation of this appeal lies in the question it raises rather than in the answer it gives. "What would Jesus do?" is a permanently valid question for one who calls himself a Christian. It cuts to the heart of the meaning of being a Christian in any age. Jesus' invitation to "follow me" either means just that or it has no coherent meaning at all.

We have a right to argue with Sheldon about his answers to the question so long as we do not try to argue the question itself out of existence or ignore its validity and urgency. We may want to rephrase it and ask, "what would Jesus have me do?" Or "what does the spirit of love nurtured by Jesus Christ lead me to do?" Or "what does loyalty to Jesus Christ require of me?"

Questions like these lie like concentric circles around the person of Jesus Christ in the life and thought of Christians. Each one looks to him for some kind of directive or guidance. If we refuse to raise any of the suggested questions, we are saying, in effect, that Jesus means nothing in terms of everyday life and problems—in which case he is irrelevant. If he means anything at all, he must mean something in particular. What does he mean? In what sense, if any, is he relevant or irrelevant to the problems we actually face? Why present him as a leader if he does not lead? Why preach Christianity as a way of life if it cannot be so interpreted?

It is the purpose of the Christian witness to throw light on questions like these. And we will have achieved a part of our purpose if we can renew and steady our vision of the glory of man and God that burst into human life and history in and through the life and teachings of Jesus Christ. We will have achieved all of our purpose if we can be reinforced in our determination to hear and heed his invitation, "Follow me."

II

Jesus Christ was no irresponsible idealist unacquainted with the problems people face. He was an active participant in the life of his day. He was an artisan, a carpenter in Nazareth, a village of Galilee. He was a workman who knew his customers as well as his tools and his craft. He knew not only the men who met the payrolls, but he knew the ones who were on them as well as the ones who needed to be on them. Farmers, fisherman, traders, soldiers and housewives were his customers. He seems to have been a most observant and sensitive participant in all that happened.

He was a responsible member of a close family circle and community. He went to the local synagogue school to be instructed in the law and the prophets of his fathers. Since Galilee was the center of revolutionary movements, he could not have escaped heated discussions as to how to cast off the yoke of Rome. The recommendations ranged all of the way from "assassination and revolution" to "let God do it."

For thirty years he lived and shared in the common life. Then came the divine summons to the public ministry. With the momentous words, "Thou art my beloved son; with thee I am well pleased" (Mark 1:11) ringing in his ears, he retired to the wilderness—an oasis in the nearby desert—to rethink the total meaning of his life and to gird himself for a new life and work.

He emerged from this solitude ready for the task. He began to preach the good news of the kingdom of God, of God's intention for life and history now brought to realization. He tried to persuade men to worship God, to consecrate themselves to the service of the Kingdom, to love and to cherish God above all else. He gathered a small group of disciples about him and endeavored to kindle their minds and spirits with his vision of the kingdom of God. He helped whomever, whenever, and wherever he could. Saint and sinner, rich and poor, adult and child, Jew and Gentile—all found a friend in him. They discovered the fact that something *new* had moved into the very center of the human situation. A new fact, a new power, a new goal—these came alive for them in Jesus Christ.

Lest we forget, he knew the meaning of bitter disappointment and apparent defeat. Not more than a handful of those who heard him preach and teach took the pains to stay with him long. Some went away sorrowing, but the large majority just went away. The crowds that came with a crown dissolved overnight into the mobs that called for his crucifixion. In the final days not even his disciples stood firm.

Criticism, opposition and naked enmity surrounded him from the very outset of his public ministry. Finally, his own family drew away from him. Respected religious leaders frowned upon him and, when he refused to be silenced by their warning, decided to silence him. Though the charge against him was obviously false, they achieved the end of getting rid of him, or so they thought.

We bear our witness to one who knew what was in man, who surely deserves to be called the Son of man as truly as the Son of God. In the Christian witness these two designations cannot be separated.[1]

---

[1] Scholars warn us that it is all but impossible to settle on some one meaning for them as used in the New Testament.

In Jesus Christ the writers of the New Testament and subsequent Christian preachers have been certain they saw the will of God for the life of man. The New Testament writers insist and agree that to grasp the meaning of Jesus Christ is to grasp the will of God for human life and, quite literally, to be given a new life in Jesus Christ. To be saved by him means to have one's old spirit replaced by a new spirit and then "to be born again."

The Christian way of life for us today will be based squarely upon the conviction that Jesus Christ links God and man in some new, mysterious, definite, and saving way. This faith we share with our fathers before us; and we seek to interpret it in a meaningful way in our own generation by making our lives bear witness to the Christian way.

III

Men bowed down with sin felt its load slip from their life, and they stood erect once more at his touch. Levi the tax collector, the harlot at the well in Samaria, the woman taken in adultery, as well as the proud, self-righteous men who gathered around to stone her—all these and many others felt the power of his confidence in their possibilities. He saw men through the eyes of love and trust because, to him, all were the children of God. He found something loveable and trustworthy in everyone. Thus he was able to be both patient with them and honest about their sins and their need for God. He combined in a remarkable way the ability to love the sinner and to flay his sin for the evil thing it is. He did this by positive rather than negative means.

Jesus knew that we cannot conquer sin merely by condemning it, much less by holding the sinner up to shame and ridicule. We can overcome sin in a life only by helping that person achieve a new level of life, one of conscious fellowship with God. And Jesus showed by his example that it is necessary to have fellowship, even as he did, with "the publicans and sinners." He not only forgave sins, but he did so in a spirit of compassion and love which identified him with the deepest needs of the sinner. He believed in and practiced the forgiveness of sins; he also had fellowship with the sinners. That, we may be sure, is one of the reasons why the religious leaders of his people were set against him. They could understand forgiveness of sins, but not fellowship with the sinner.

It is the serious and considered judgment of Christian history that in and through him, God was working and continues to work these mighty acts of transformation and redemption in human life and history. We see and celebrate the meaning of this redemptive activity in great figures like the apostle Paul and John Wesley. We see it also in the tens of millions of others whose names we do not know. They are persons whose lives show that they follow the Christ.

Jesus Christ continues to challenge men by placing the highest possible valuation on us. He has called us the children of God and confronted us with the highest possible expectation for our life: to live as a child of God. He continues to make the most wonderful offer imaginable—to show us the way and to lead us in the task of realizing in our own daily life God's intention in and for us. He seems to have faced, at least in principle, every sort of problem we are called on to face. He does not ask us to do things that he has not done himself. He leads us by what he does as truly as by what he says. Today, as in the first century, when men undergo this miracle of redemption through fellowship with Jesus Christ, they say with the centurion: "Truly this man was a Son of God." (Mark 15:39.)

IV

Our witness to him as the way may be phrased in still another way: In him we discover both an awareness of the power of the love of God and complete confidence in it.

Jesus is the most completely God-conscious and God-trustful person we know. In him we see the will of God molding the life of man. His life and teachings exhibit an unparalleled sensitivity to the reality and activity of God. Touch him at any point of his life, and we are stunned by the measure of his consecration to the will of God. The witness of the New Testament is that he walked with God daily and God blessed him with authority and power.

He was utterly unafraid of defeat and death. He knew that the opposition of men might delay but could never defeat the will of God. He believed that a life lost in God was found of God through all eternity. In life and in death, the power of the love of God in the face of every problem and every difficulty was, to him, the supreme fact and would have the final word. His was the love that conquers death for us, for our loved ones, and for the causes we hold dear. It is a love that yields us a cosmic home, a love that will not let us go. It is a love in whose wide-ranging concern the stars find their courses and the very hairs on our head are numbered. It is a love that comes to us not as an emotion to be enjoyed but as a life to be lived, a work to be done, a world to be built.

The invitation to discipleship still stands: "Follow me." When a Hindu student was asked to describe the meaning of the Christian witness he said, "If you follow Christ three things will happen to you: first, you will be delivered from all fears; second, you will be absurdly happy; third, you will have trouble."

3

The Church and Our Witness

I

THE CHRISTIAN faith and the Christian ethic are dependent upon the Christian fellowship. This is a way of saying that one cannot be a Christian without being a churchman. If this comes as a blow to many of our contemporaries, they need to be reminded that the question of whether one could be a Christian without being a churchman was not even asked until a hundred years ago. If you were a Christian, you were in the Christian church. When the great Reformation movements were under way on the continent and in England, men did not move away from the church into no church; they moved into another church. Martin Luther, John Calvin, and John Wesley were very explicit on this point. Calvin said, "A departure from the church is a renunciation of God and Christ." Wesley said, "There is no such thing as a solitary Christian." Judgments like these have the solid support of the New Testament.

This is clearly so throughout the Gospels. Christ's call to men was always a call to enter in and to become an integral part of his followers in the new community. While he never forgot and repeatedly emphasized the inner pole of religious faith, the first overt consequent of belief in him was to leave

all and follow him in company with other believers. Bishop
Charles Gore had the facts before him when he wrote, "There
is nothing more central in the mind of Christ than that you
can only love God in fellowship."

It was unthinkable to Christians in New Testament times
that one could be a Christian without belonging to the Christian fellowship. A Christian was one who had been called
into that fellowship by Christ; he had been set apart from
the world, but set apart as a member of a fellowship which
itself was set apart by Christ. He was not called into "splendid
isolation"; he was called into a "household of faith"; he was
called to become one of "a people of God."

Paul's letters ring with exhortations that underscore this
position. He urges his readers to bear one another's burdens,
to let the needs of others be guides in their own conduct, to
strengthen the weak, to counsel the erring, to judge the
quarrelsome, to conduct themselves in a respectable manner
in their gatherings, to share in meeting the needs of food
and shelter for the faithful. Read Romans 16, if there is
doubt about the earthy, human nature of the early Christian
community.

Even a casual reading of the New Testament will demon-
strate how fundamental the Christian fellowship was to the
early Christians. It was sacramental through and through;
that is, it dealt with sacred mysteries. It was presided over
by the Holy Spirit, and it was blessed by the actual presence
of Christ himself. You entered it through the rite of baptism
administered by the elders of the group. You celebrated the
sacrifices of our Lord by the rite of the Eucharist, or the
Lord's Supper, in company with other believers. You wor-
shiped God in fellowship with others.

You studied the Scriptures and heard expositions of them
as members one of another. You shared your possessions in

proportion to the needs of others. You married within the fellowship. You accepted the guidance of the fellowship. You suffered as a member of it whenever persecution came upon it. In the hour of your death, the visible community slowly faded and the invisible community of the saints came into view, and you became one with them.

Should one want to separate Christianity from church membership, he might as well forget the New Testament in his search for proof. It would only embarrass him to turn anywhere in those sacred pages.

II

The Christian tradition has continued to accept and insist upon the New Testament understanding of the necessary connection between the individual Christian and the Christian community. To be a Christian—a follower of Jesus Christ—necessarily means to believe, to love, and to seek to serve him. While these are deeply personal matters, it is not possible for an individual to do any one of them on his own. Though they touch the wellsprings of thought, feeling, and moral commitment of each individual, they are as profoundly social as any conviction or enterprise could conceivably be.

Take the matter of believing in Jesus Christ. Will even the most confirmed individualist claim that he can do this unassisted by anyone else? We would not even know of Christ had it not been for the church—the fellowship of the faithful who gathered around him as disciples. Later on that fellowship gathered around the disciples and apostles as continuing witnesses; and still later, members of the early church wrote and cherished the New Testament itself. The church alone has made it possible for us to know about him, let alone believe in him. Basically, what we do in the church is a finger pointing at this fact—the fact of Jesus Christ, and his claim upon men.

It is equally impossible to love him on our own, apart from all others; that is, if we are going to mean by love what he meant by it. He was not talking about an esthetic yearning for beauty or truth when he spoke of love. To love God, as he meant it, is to identify oneself with the will and work of God in life, among people. To love one's neighbor, as he meant it, is to identify oneself with the needs and the welfare of the neighbor, no matter who he might be. Love, as Jesus understood it, is the very antithesis of drawing apart from others. Rather, it is the endless quest for an ever deeper relationship with them. This is far from easy. It may begin, as one sly but discerning critic put it, with an effort "to love my crooked neighbor with all my crooked heart," but it cannot rest content until men stretch hands of faith and love toward each other saying, "We are one in Christ."

His final word to the disciples—the Great Commission: "Go therefore and make disciples of all nations"—can hardly be construed as an adventure in isolationism or individualism. We cannot serve him who gave himself for others unless we are willing to become one with all who love and seek to serve him.

III

Certain facts ought to be kept before the person who thinks it may be possible to be a Christian without being a member of the Christian fellowship. The first is this: Some kind of religious organization is essential to vital religion. It is an historical fact that all vital religion expresses itself in and through some kind of historical and institutional tradition. But for that tradition the insights of faith would have perished. The church has perpetuated these insights and thereby has made them available to subsequent generations.

It is one thing to say that religion is intensely personal, and quite another to say that it is, therefore, a private matter. Religion is concerned with our relationships with other people and with God. One way we gauge the importance of work in art, science, and literature is whether or not it has expressed itself in schools, traditions or institutions. One token of the importance of religion (though not the only one) is its historic determination to insert itself as a social and institutional force in the unfolding life of mankind.

The purpose of the church, as the late Dean Willard Sperry once said, is to "make God real to every generation." It does this by incorporating its teachings and institutions in a tradition called the Christian fellowship. It is a matter of historical record that the church has performed its task with some measure of real success. It has done more than simply survive the ravages of time; it has grown and spread until it is one of the most important facts in human history. It has crossed the borders and barriers that usually separate men from each other—clan, race, nation and culture. Though it has taken on (and cast off) many different social forms, the purpose of and in each one was the ancient goal of the disciples: to preach Christ to all men. The real marvel of the church is not the existence of so many different social forms of expression, but the continuing fidelity of each form to the single purpose of the Christian faith.

The Christian fellowship, then, has been and is "the carrier" of religious faith from one generation to another as well as from one culture to another. Were it not for this fellowship there is no reason to think that the Christian faith would have survived the first generation of witnesses. But it not only survived; it grew swiftly and began to bear fruit everywhere.

Although there are many different church forms, each one exhibits what might be called a fourfold ministry.

IV

First, there is the ministry of worship. The church both practices and cultivates the practice of the worship of God. That is the true foundation of her purpose, the true meaning of her life, and there can be no Christian faith without it. The church is not an end in herself; she is the means to the end of receiving, interpreting, and sharing the will of God with other men. Formal services of public worship do not serve their purpose unless they enable each participant to glimpse anew the glory of God which is trying to burst through the hymns, the Scripture, the prayer, and the sermon.

The purpose of worship is simple: to galvanize men into action in the name, for the sake, and in the service of God as we see him in Jesus Christ. Worship is an earnest effort to confront God; it is man humbly but courageously trying to think God's thoughts after him, trying to get some clearer insight into his will in order that he may make it the will of his life. It is a matter of simple historical record that the public worship of God has proved to be an indispensable instrument in the nurture of vital Christianity.

A second ministry is the ministry of education. This is necessary work for an institution which tries to bring nearly three thousand years of human experience to bear on our problems today. The Bible is the central document in continuing our religious tradition and in guiding a person in the Christian life. Only one who has never studied it seriously can think it simple, easily understood, and a quite teachable book. It is no easy task to establish the relevance of biblical teachings to many of the problems we face today; yet the effort must be made. To do this requires knowledge of the Bible and an accurate understanding of the problems that are harassing us today. Even one who tries to be a Christian "in splendid isolation" from the Christian fellowship finds himself dependent upon Christian scholars and teachers, who make possible the food on which he feasts, as he sits alone in his private corner.

The ministry of fellowship is still another ministry of the church. Historically, the church began in the homes of the faithful. The ministry of fellowship which began there continues to be an indispensable part of the church's work. We are social beings; we were not meant to live alone, but in intimate communion with each other. When, for any reason, the bonds that bind us to any given group are severed, instead of being freed, we more frequently feel lost.

The church to be true to her vision must extend the mantle of her fellowship to all men evenly. A church that confines its membership to one class, one race, or one nation is a contradiction. In so doing it attempts to include some and exclude others of the human family from the fellowship of the church. The church must include all or surrender her claim to be a Christian church.

A final movement is to be found in the church's ministry of social conscience. The church's call to this ministry has seldom received a more effective statement than that of the Lambeth Conference of the Protestant Episcopal Church in 1948: "The church is the champion of man against all that cheapens and degrades him; for the Gospel is the charter of man's dignity. The mission of the church now as always is to proclaim and live out the Gospel by which alone men can be saved from sin and judgment, and the world from despair and self-destruction . . . we must bring the teachings and the example of Christ into our everyday life . . . nothing that is good in the sight of God should be outside the church's interest."

So far from being the concern of a few socially-minded church leaders, these sentiments reflect broad-gauge trends within and among the churches of Christendom. Every major church nourishes and is nourished by a "social creed" which endeavors to articulate the Christian responsibility regarding the social issues of the day. Both the National and the World Council of Churches are endeavoring to help Christians understand the meaning of a Christian society and a Christian world. To this end, they study all problems that tend to separate man from man.

The Christian church owes the world an example of a fellowship that actually heals the wounds and bridges the chasms that separate us from each other. To do this the church must lift her common life to the highest possible levels of brotherhood, compassion, and love. Instead of being an extension and passive extenuation of prejudices and divisions, the Christian fellowship should rebuke the world at the point of serious division by the demonstration of unity and fellowship. The church's most effective critique of the sins of the world will not be what she says; it will be what she is and does. And the church that does not criticize the world for conscience' sake will soon find that she has lost both her conscience and the desire to criticize anyone for any reason.

Let it be noted that the Christian fellowship is working hard toward these great ends. We are learning how to work together; we have come a long way already, but a longer road stretches ahead. We shall be doing nothing more important as a church than giving encouragement and support to further progress in developing a quality of living that is worthy to be called Christian.

4

The Kingdom and Its Claims

I

THE CHRISTIAN ethic is the Christian faith come alive in human life. If we touch the Christian church anywhere in her historic career, we lay hands on something in motion. She is not a static entity that can be satisfactorily and finally described in terms of any given period or event. Rather, the church is dynamic, its rich reality includes what is and also what is to be. The amazingly comprehensive and profound activity of the church is never mere motion; it is an honest and determined effort to serve one purpose—the kingdom of God.

Secular-minded historians have their trouble trying to understand the church. They attempt to chronicle the influence of the church in and on history without taking the trouble to grasp the fundamental meaning of the kingdom of God to the church and in the life of her people.

It is a good axiom for historians and all other students of behavior to know the purpose, the goal, or the motive of an action in order to understand it. It is not enough to describe what the church has been and done: we must be able to say why she has attempted and continues to attempt to do it. The kingdom of God is the *why* that will help us understand

the *what* of Christian life and history. He who would understand history must be alert to these factors. They have a
very far-reaching significance.

As people of the Christian faith seek to bear witness today,
they must take seriously the ancient commitment to the
kingdom of God. Only so can they make their greatest contribution toward the salvation of the world.

From the beginning of Christian history, the supreme end
of Christian life and work has been the kingdom of God.
Without it the Christian gospel is a clarion call to nothing in
particular. It is the end, and the only end, plainly prefigured
in the kind of life Jesus recommended to his disciples. The
startling ethical principles of the Sermon on the Mount
are means aimed at the end of the kingdom of God and
toward no other end known to man. That is why it is of
utmost importance to clarify our thinking on the basic meaning of the kingdom of God both in the New Testament and
in terms of Christian experience.

II

Both John the Baptist and Jesus of Nazareth began their
public life with an announcement of the imminence of the
kingdom of God. There was real confusion among their
hearers as to what they meant since several conceptions of
the Kingdom were in circulation at the time. The Gospels
spend much time seeking to clarify what is meant by the
"kingdom of God." Careful scholars assure us that several
meanings are clearly evident in the Gospels. In fact, one
careful survey of the several meanings concludes with these
measured words: "From this survey it is readily seen that
the term 'kingdom of God (or heaven)' in the usage of Jesus
is not easy to be defined; that it appears to be an elastic,

poetic symbol rather than the vehicle of a single, sharply-bounded conception." Having lifted this warning, the writer proceeds with the judgment that the fundamental thought in the term "kingdom of God" may be phrased in some such fashion as this: "Where the will of God is done, there the kingdom of God has come. . . . Accordingly . . . the fundamental idea of 'kingdom of heaven' is the *rule of God*."[1]

Two claims keep recurring in the various interpretations of the kingdom of God in the New Testament.

It is God's kingdom. It is not Caesar's or man's; it outranks these in every way. Citizens of the Kingdom will be those whose wills are moved by God's will. The Kingdom will be both theocentric (centered in God) and theocratic (ruled by God). Humility and obedience are the only open doors to it. Thus the penitent publican of Jesus' parable "went down to his house justified," while his proud companion stood outside and alone. Jesus' own humility in the presence of God's will is forever instructive. That is why he taught unnumbered millions to pray, "Thy kingdom come. Thy will be done in earth, as it is in heaven."

Fundamental in the idea of the kingdom of God is this: Evil is removed and God is revealed as Saviour of his people. In short; the kingdom of God is the perfect rule of God.

The kingdom of God, then, is a condition in life when God's will is understood and fulfilled. This condition exists *ideally* at any given time short of its realization, much as the docking of a boat in port exists ideally until it is actually there. But this fulfillment is not to be forced upon us in spite of ourselves. If it is ever achieved, whether in personal or social living, it will be because people like us accept the claim of the Kingdom and bear witness of their loyalty to it.

[1] James Hastings and J. A. Selbie, *A Dictionary of Christ and the Gospels* (New York, Charles Scribner's Sons, 1906), I, pages 932-33. Used by permission.

III

Another basic fact about this Kingdom is that *it is the power of God, the will of God, actively at work in human life and affairs through incarnation in the lives of people.*

Politically-minded people usually interpret it in political terms—with the Messiah supplanting the Caesars for early Christians or a world government supplanting the international anarchy of national governments in the minds of many today. Ecclesiastically-minded people interpret it in terms of church thought and life. They anticipate the day when the churches of the world will be "one church" and the further day when the church will have completed her task of being the instrument of God in the redemption of the world. Ethically-minded people think of the Kingdom as a world in which justice and brotherhood prevail; they feel that men and women are called to God to bend every effort in this direction.

Although this Kingdom seems strange by ordinary standards, we recognize it because certain tokens add to its strangeness, but they also underscore its importance in human life.

For in this Kingdom love ultimately wins the victory over hate, truth over falsehood, and peace over war. Although we have never even been close to victories like these, people of the Christian faith continue to believe it is possible to achieve them. Christians continue to preach and to work for them as being the only ultimately important victories open to us.

The kingdom of God is the kingdom of love—the Kingdom in which love reigns supreme in life. Where God is, love is; where love is not, God is not. We who call ourselves "Christian" should be familiar with that inescapable inference from our historic conviction that "God is love." If we take that insight with any degree of seriousness, we will never again say that the kingdom of God is an affair of another world. It belongs to this world in the literal and exact sense that it gives us a vision of the real meaning of the purpose of God in history. He is trying to build a world where love will reign supreme in human relationships. In that world, love will have overcome hate, and the result will be a far stranger world than we have ever known. Yet our greatest spirits have dreamed about it. We have all longed for something like it. We have sung about that

> ". . . one great fellowship of love
> Through-out the whole wide earth."

In the kingdom of God, truth will be off the scaffold and will reign triumphant in the human mind and spirit. It staggers our imagination even to try to visualize a world free of all the accidental, incidental, and wholly intentional kinds of deception that go on all the time. To be freed from the necessity of pretense; to be fit and able to think, speak and act openly; to be transparently loyal to all that is true, beautiful and of good report—that would be Paradise Restored!

The Kingdom is the sovereignty of truth as well. There is an unseverable connection between faith in God and faith in truth. One of the distinctive tokens of his Kingdom will be the demonstration of that in our common life. The kingdom of God is the kingdom in which love and truth are the goals toward which we strive, the road on which we walk; indeed, love and truth supply us with the strength to keep on the journey.

The kingdom of God will be a condition of peace. We have believed in the possibility of that for thousands of years. Isaiah dreamed of the day when "the wolf also shall dwell with the lamb, and the leopard shall lie down with the kid"

(Isaiah 11:6) ; when "they shall beat their swords into plow-shares, and their spears into pruninghooks;" when "nation shall not lift up sword against nation, neither shall they learn war any more." (Isaiah 2:4, Revised Standard Version.)

No extended argument is necessary to convince this generation that the kingdom of God, so conceived, is the difference between life and death for our civilization. It is not a glorious dream painted on the clouds of grim reality by the setting sun of human hope; it is a real and powerful alternative goal for human striving.

The kingdom of God is as real as an ideal. It is as real to Christians as the idea of the port of destination is to the captain of a ship at sea. Although he cannot see it, he steers for it. Without it as the destination, he has neither need nor notion of a right direction.

How real is the ideal of their marriage to a young couple taking their vows at the altar of a church? What are their plans, hopes, and dreams for their shared life in marriage, home, and family over the years ahead? Is not this ideal the most real thing about their marriage? If they have a high and radiant ideal, they will have a port of destination, and they will find the will and strength needed to manage the problems that present themselves over the years. Though the ideal is by no means the detailed answer to each problem they must face, it will enable them to face all problems with confidence in each other and in their marriage.

The kingdom of God is the ideal by which we measure the worth of what we are and do, individually and collectively. Believing it to be God's purpose for life, we are ready to measure ourselves by it, to bend ourselves to conform to it. With it as a vivid reality in our thinking we have a sense of direction; without it we are like a captain without a port of destination.

The kingdom of God is as powerful as a purpose. Man is or can be guided by a great purpose; one in which he believes, one to which he commits his life, and one for which he will die if need be. In the Christian faith, the highest, holiest vision we have of such a purpose is the kingdom of God—that strange kingdom where love, truth, and peace will prevail.

For the kingdom of God is a life to be lived, a work to be done, a destiny to be fulfilled. It is a new life—our present life redeemed and renewed by a humble and sincere appreciation of God's will for life as we see it in Jesus Christ. It is a work to be done—since the steadiest emphases in the teachings of Jesus are calls to action, work, and duty. It is a destiny to be fulfilled because man's life can unfold; because man can never know the meaning of the good, the abundant life except as he seeks to be a fit citizen of the Kingdom.

The kingdom of God is the frame of reference for all our thinking and living when we think and live as Christians. And what a difference it does make! At a stroke, it delivers us from the grip of parochial concerns, provincial plans, and preoccupation with fragmentary interests. Race, nation, church, our "way of life"—all these nearer gods of human history become the half-gods they actually are when placed against the background of the kingdom of God.

As the late William Temple was fond of saying, "The kingdom of God is the sovereignty of love." This is a singularly acute way of stating an age-old conception of the kingdom of God. Better than anything else, it drives home the fact that the kingdom of God is not an other-worldly affair; it belongs to this world in the literal and exact sense that it serves as the ethical standard by which we measure our motives, plans, and deeds. By so doing, the kingdom of God places upon man the unmistakable stamp of divine worth and eternal destiny, for God loves man with a love that out-

distances our most far-ranging hopes. God trusts man to hear
and heed his will for life and history, and to become a co-
worker with him in the redemption of the world. This
conception of the ultimate nature of the universe and human
history is the firm foundation for Christian ethics—an ethics,
let it be underscored, that aims at nothing less, and can be
satisfied with nothing less, than new men, a new order of
society, and a new direction for human history.

Convictions like these about the nature and the meaning
of the kingdom of God are not and cannot be presented as
blueprints for specific and detailed changes to be made
throughout society. They will, however, if and to the degree
that they are taken seriously, keep Christians everlastingly
at the task of trying to discover the outlines of such blueprints.
Only three types of persons can seriously object to this effort:
one who thinks the world cannot be improved, one who thinks
the kingdom of God is already here, and one who thinks the
Kingdom was not meant to be relevant to human life and
history. All other Christians will fall to the task of fulfilling
the vision of the kingdom of God in terms of themselves,
their comrades, and human history.

Our belief in the kingdom of God means that as God lives,
our hope and peace lie in his will and nowhere else.

IV

The word "reconciliation" suggests the strategy by which
we seek to do the work of the Kingdom in our life and time.
It comes to us from Paul's famous description: "All this is
from God, who through Christ reconciled us to himself and
gave us the ministry of reconciliation." (2 Corinthians 5:18,
R.S.V.) The whole idea of reconciliation, according to Paul,
grows out of the profound religious experience of having

found God's will and purpose for life in Jesus Christ. It is well to remember that reconciliation originates in the activity of divine love, not in the reasoned projects of men. If we separate it from its proper source, it will wither away into a set of futile compromises. If we keep it in touch with that source, it will persist until men are actually reconciled with God and with each other.

The nature of reconciliation is integrally related to the whole system of ideas that constitute the Christian view of life. It rests upon the deeper and broader beliefs in the nature of God as love, in his will as we see it in Jesus Christ, and in his claim on us as we feel it in the kingdom of God. Only as we have experienced the reconciling love of God have we anything to bear witness to in the name of reconciliation.

Reconciliation is not so much an idea as it is an experience which we are attempting to share with others. We attempt to share it in ways that are congenial with its own nature. The aim of reconciliation is to achieve peace and further community in human life and relations. One who would be an instrument of the love of God in the ministry of reconciliation will find himself involved in four basic movements or steps.

Obviously, the first movement is toward God and the re-dedication of one's life to the kingdom of God. We must keep before us the reality of the love of God, believing it to be the only fundamental and truly eternal fact in the world. We must seek to find his will and his way for our lives and for the conflicts that are within us and around us.

The second movement is to be completely sensitive to both sides in a dispute or conflict. For there are always two sides, notwithstanding the obvious fact that neither side thinks so. Effective reconciliation requires that the values of both sides be known and preserved as far as this can be done. There is no place for the partisan frame of mind relative to the dispute in the process of reconciliation. A Christian advocates neither side but seeks to understand both.

This leads to the third movement, namely, we must be carefully and sympathetically critical of the contesting claims in any disputes. We are not called upon to beat whatever drums are thrust in our hands in a moment of social turmoil. If we would serve the God of all, we must be as objective as possible about the claims advanced in conflict. For we are called of God to try to bring his judgment to bear upon life through the process of reconciliation.

The final movement in the process of Christian reconciliation requires that we shall be in the battle, yet above it. The only effective agent in the process of healing a conflict is the person who belongs to both parties, yet belongs to neither. Almost from the beginning of our tradition Christians have realized that they are supposed to be in the world and yet not of it. It is the calling of the Christian to try to lift both parties involved in a dispute to a higher level of understanding concerning the real values at stake. We need to remember how Jesus went to stormy Jerusalem against the most tearful entreaties of his disciples who urged him to make his witness in a safe place.

When Gandhi wanted to quell the riots in India he took up his residence at the heart of the most turbulent area and opened his fast. When Dr. Martin Luther King of Montgomery, Alabama, led his crusade against segregation, he did not come to the relative security of the northern part of the United States. He stayed in his home town and sought to lead the white people and the Negroes alike to a new level of awareness concerning the reality and power of love as the only basis for reconciliation.

The Christian will not and cannot be an outsider looking in on the conflicts of the world; he will be a part of the situation sharing to the fullest possible extent, particularly at those points where he can help to conserve the greatest values of life. And he does so, not for his own sake, but for God's sake.

V

As we seek to bear our witness through the spirit of reconciliation, we need to remember that the healing work of God's love in human life makes it possible. We do not heal; God does that. But we can help men turn toward God. Reconciliation has not been fully realized when we "get the idea across." It is realized when a new relationship has actually been built; when a new structure of life has been introduced into human relations; when there is a new pattern of personality or social relationships in existence. Reconciliation is a way of healing conflicts and building peace in place of tension, fear, and war.

When World War II was drawing to its conclusion, one of the political leaders of this country, speaking to a group of churchmen, said, "How I envy you men when this war is over! You will be able to go across any battle line on the face of the earth with hand outstretched and the word 'brother' on your lips, and you will meet someone coming across in the same spirit from the other side. That is the real foundation for world peace." His insight into the peculiar advantage of the Christian faith should effectively rebuke the feeling on the part of churchmen that they must react first as citizens and secondly as Christians. To step within the Christian fold is to assume the primacy of the Christian gospel. And that is the gospel of reconciliation.

As we set ourselves to the tremendous task laid upon us by this ministry, there is real strength in the knowledge that we are but instruments in the love of God as he seeks to work his perfect work in the world. What we try to do is not done simply and solely in our own wisdom and strength, for we are taking our course of life and effort from the will of God as we see it in Jesus Christ. We have no alternative in this matter. As Emile Cammaerts said, "Christianity is the story of the redemption of man, through the love of God, or it is nothing." If we are not willing to assume the ministry of reconciliation, we have no Christian ministry, however useful a purpose we may seem to serve in the promotion of racial, class, and national interests.

In reply to the direct question "Should the Christian church advocate policies of reconciliation in terms of specific social conflict?" only one answer is permitted. Yes, the church should advocate such policies if she believes reconciliation to be God's way of overcoming enmity, if she is prepared to lead out, to show the way, to level down the hills and fill up the valleys of difficulties, prejudices, and inequities which exist. Yet we always come back to the question: Are we willing to accept the ministry of reconciliation as the supreme work of the love of God in and through our life individually and collectively? If we are not, it is a serious question as to whether we have any distinctly Christian ministry at all. This sobering fact will cause all of us to reappraise ourselves in the light of this responsibility.

CHAPTER

5

Temperance

I

THE WORD "temperance" has found it difficult to retain the wealth of its original meaning. In our time it is linked almost exclusively with the cause of moral control in the use of alcoholic beverages, and it is rapidly becoming a synonym for abstinence, or the complete refusal to drink alcoholic beverages in any form or amount. This, of course, is the official position of The Methodist Church.

There was a time when "temperance" had a magnificent sweep of meaning not only among the Greeks but in our own religious heritage. Some of the synonyms for temperance illustrate the richness of its background: moderation, sobriety, forebearance, self-denial, self-restraint, self-control.

Temperance, broadly conceived, is essential to the Christian way of life. A brief survey of its meaning will indicate why this is so.

II

Temperance comes from a Latin word which means "proportion." It was used to convey a certain view of life cherished by the Greeks and adopted by the Romans. The

47

Greeks loved life, but one kind of life above all others: life under control; life in balance. It was with their ethics as with their art: nothing too much. Their best thinkers made this sort of life the *summum bonum*, the ideal of ethics and morals. It was a life blessed by harmony and proportion, with nothing too much. It was a life in which the higher faculties of spirit and mind controlled the lower faculties of appetite, instinct, and emotion. For the Greeks, the temperate life, the life under the control of reason and judgment, was the ideal.

The people of the Old Testament believed in temperance just as devoutly as the Greeks, but with a significant difference. Where the Greeks exalted the ideal of a life under the control of reason, the Hebrews exalted a life under the control of the law, the will of God as revealed in the Torah. The Hebrews' word for this relationship was "righteousness."

But the difference in names must not obscure a fundamental similarity in meaning. The Hebrews were committed to a life under the control of God's will, and they were not content with general principles. The rabbis spelled out this commitment with detailed care, describing how the day should be spent, what food might be eaten, what clothing should be worn, what work might be done. The life of the righteous man was one of order and discipline; it was controlled by perfect obedience to the law.

The early Christians were good Jews in this regard. They too sought to live a disciplined and controlled life. Paul believed that the true miracle of the Christian experience occurs when Christ actually enters a man's life, and gives him a new heart and a new spirit and makes of him a new creature.

The Christian life, from the beginning, has been a life under the discipline of love, of loyalty to Jesus Christ. No writer of the New Testament thought that a person achieved such discipline easily. It was Paul who said that he felt an actual war inside him as he sought to bring his stubborn, sinful will, mind, and flesh under the control of Christ. Sometimes, try as he might, he was not successful. "I do not understand my own actions," (Romans 7:15) he confessed. "For I do not do the good I want, but the evil I do not want is what I do." (Romans 7:19, Revised Standard Version.) Small wonder the early church tried to develop techniques for subjugating the flesh to the spirit. Sometimes alone in the desert, sometimes in groups banded together to help each other "overcome the flesh and the world," they sought to live a life under control of complete loyalty to Christ.

This is the true impulse which brought a stream of special religious orders into being over the centuries. Wanting to live a religious life of the highest, purest, most disciplined order, they chose this way to do it. Whatever we may think of the wisdom of their choice, we will want to honor the sincerity and loyalty of their call. They have set their minds and lives on "things above," and they seek to serve them with complete devotion.

However much we may question the means they use, we cannot and do not question the end they seek. That is binding upon all Christians—a life of perfect obedience to Christ. The Christian life is one lived in open and conscious loyalty to Jesus Christ. It will be characterized by love, compassion, forgiveness, and patience. This is the continuing meaning of temperance in Christian ethics.

III

This notion of a life under the control of a great central loyalty to Jesus Christ rises up to rebuke the casual, easygoing way we are tempted to live these days!

Each one will have to make confession for himself, but it is easy to see lives without the discipline of a great, creative loyalty. There are little loyalties—short-term loyalties, we might call them—and they take over. Such lives are not so much out of control as they are under the control of loyalties that distort them.

This is how it works—or can work. We all believe in freedom—a maximum of freedom for an individual to think, to read, to live as he chooses, limited only by the welfare of the group. Two men, sharing this same belief, may react differently. One lets his appetites take over his reason and judgment, and he becomes a drunkard, glutton, or libertine. The other, thinking of himself as a child of God, feels called to live a life worthy of that faith. One joins the cult of sensuality and obscenity that has so many devotees these days; the other rejects this cult and joins instead the fellowship of those who see and seek the things that are above.

It is a disturbing thing to read widely in the novels and short stories these days, particularly the best selling paperback books. Granted at once, emotion, appetite, instinct, and sexual interest are essential parts of human life and are, therefore, legitimate concerns for the artist. But does this admission cast off all restraint and controls, and deliver us without protest or defense into the deluge of sensualism and obscenity that floods so much of our life and literature today? No one expects a war novel to be written in the language used to describe a little girl's birthday party, but does this fact excuse the glorification of brutality and the obvious enjoyment of sensuality that are so characteristic of nearly all pseudo-war novels of our time?

Much as we fear censorship in any form, some people are beginning to wonder about the present trend. If it continues, we could be forced to reopen the possibility that censorship in some form may be necessary. Lest this be regarded as the professional opinion of the clergy, consider these lines from a book review that Dorothy Parker wrote of two current novels: ". . . though censorship seems to be an unwieldy and eventually a corrupt business, I do wish that something could be done to stop this dreary flow of dirt to the printed page."

But why be hard on the writers? Are they not giving us what we really want? How else can we account for the phenomenal popularity of their productions? A successful novelist, when asked for his formula, put it with brutal simplicity: "Hate and sex; hate and sex." A few years ago a British writer said that the clue to a successful film lay in the vivid suggestion of fornication, adultery, or rape, with a killing or two thrown in for good measure.

We have no desire to interfere with the freedom of the husky-voiced stars of movie and television fame when we express concern for the moral fiber of our children, youth, and adults who assist in their glorification. So many of these individuals have let their lives get out of control. And quite literally they are lost in the whirlwind of their own emotions. So also are the lives of those who glorify them. We cannot play with the wild winds of intemperance without having to battle the disasters they bring.

Social studies have been warning us of the rapid rise of juvenile delinquency in all forms, especially the abnormal increase in the number of pregnancies and abortions among unmarried girls of high school age.

Few of us would lay all blame for this on the movies. The blame lies in what can only be called a new era of intemperance, of life without a central loyalty strong enough to discipline and control appetite and emotion. Hollywood is simply a vivid symbol of the casual, easy-going way in which this new era is willing to overlook, if not glorify, the evils of

sensuality, intemperance, and of life that refuses to accept
the need for moral discipline. It is no accident that the cults
of brutality and sensuality among us—especially among our
young people—take for their heroes the moral derelicts of
the screen.

Each year churches are asked to set aside one week and
designate it as "Youth Temperance Education Week." This
is all to the good, but why limit it to youth? What about their
parents? The youth have learned their intemperance from
those who are adults. For every week dedicated to the education of youth for temperance, there should be at least ten
weeks devoted to the education of adults on this same matter.

Yet it will do little or no good to set aside time in any
amount for this purpose, if we will not face up to the basic
meaning of temperance. Temperance means the disciplining
of life by a central loyalty. And for the Christian it means the
disciplining of life by loyalty to Jesus Christ.

IV

This may seem a dreary prospect to some and, in a way,
it is. It reminds us of what Dr. Paul Scherer once said of
John Calvin's stern ethics: "Calvin could not stop sin, but
he could take all of the fun out of it."

That suggests one of the things the Christian faith is trying
to do in life. It seeks to throw the light of fair, disciplined
judgment on the things that degrade and destroy. It seeks
to set our minds on "things above" that will lead to the more
abundant life. The Christian faith helps one to bring all of
life under the discipline of a great loyalty to Jesus Christ.

The Christian faith does not seek to take the fun out of
life, but it does try to find enjoyment in activities and relationships that are decent, honorable, and creative. It neither

ignores nor treats as sinful the honest emotions of sex—for they are given to us by God—but it does seek their fulfillment in the enduring relationships of marriage, home, and family, rather than in fugitive affairs that cheapen and degrade all concerned. It recognizes the deep emotional equipment that gives rise to hatred, anger, fear, and prejudices. It seeks to redirect those emotions so they can find expression in attitudes and deeds of love—for love without deep feeling is a word, nothing more. When life is lived at its best, love seeks and finds expression in understanding, concern, compassion, and forgiveness.

The intemperate man is one whose life balloons out around some one appetite or emotion. He has lost all sense of proportion, and all moral and spiritual control of life. His only salvation is to give himself to something so much greater than himself, his little satisfactions, and momentary triumphs, that he will become a new person. This points to a costly victory, but it can be won. The way toward it is open to all. The biggest reason why it can be won is that God is trying to help us. We are not alone in our struggle for a life under the control of loyalty to Jesus Christ, for God is with us. We are not alone as we seek to see and to serve "things above"—*for there are things above*—placed there by God and revealed to us by him in Jesus Christ.

When we think of a Christian, we do not think of a man who is infallible, for none is that. Nor do we think of one who is perfect, for all make mistakes. But we do think of one who consciously, openly, and joyfully sets his mind on the "things above." Those things are found in Christ, and the Christian conscientiously and faithfully seeks them for himself and for others. Such a person is blessed by a life under control, because he gives his loyalty to Christ and Christ gives him the power for right living. He will be able to say with Paul, "I can do all things through Christ which strengtheneth me." (Philippians 4:13.)

Dick Shepard had it right when he said, "Christianity consists not in abstaining from doing things no gentlemen would think of doing, but in doing things that are unlikely to occur to anyone who is not in touch with the Spirit of Christ."

This is the meaning of a life under the control of Jesus Christ. It begins with the management of one's own self. It spreads inevitably to the sharing of the "things that are above" throughout the whole range of society.

6

Family Relations

I

WHEN we say we must have a Christian home as the foundation of a Christian civilization, we face one of the gravest problems of our time. The Christian home is having a hard time of it. The leaping divorce rate; the Kinsey reports on the frequency of marital infidelity and the easy rationalizations that people make; the almost casual view we now take of marriage and divorce; the enormous increase in juvenile delinquency as a result of broken homes—all these are sobering facts. They point to the widespread waning of any serious effort on the part of many people to have homes and families that daily express the Christian way of life.

More hinges on our efforts to steady and strengthen the Christian quality of living in family and home than we would like to think. Statesmen, no matter how wise, devout, and well-intentioned they may be, cannot of themselves create a Christian civilization. Their decisions and policies, while of great importance, are limited by the basic spiritual materials and relationships with which they must work. To ask a Christian statesman to strive for a Christian world, supported by 600,000,000 fitful, wavering, compromising, half-convinced Christians, is manifestly to ask the impossible.

The true gauge of one's desire to have a Christian civilization is found in the kind of person he is. What kind of family and home are you trying to build? How sincere and thorough is your commitment to the will of God as made manifest in the life and teachings of Jesus Christ?

II

What does it mean to let the Christian way of life express itself in and through a Christian family and home?

The answer to this question need not be abstract. It can be as concrete, as human, as near at hand as every home. It is as concrete as the conversations over the breakfast tables on any given morning, or as the plans that are laid for today and tomorrow. The Christian way expresses itself in the way we meet successes and reverses in daily living, in our contacts with our neighbors, and in our ability to cope with the small as well as the great decisions that must be made each day. A Christian home, like every other adventure that bears the name Christian, is a way of life with an ideal, a standard at its center. As we understand and accept this ideal as the goal of life, we are on our way toward achieving it. A Christian home does not just happen; it is the result of a serious and sustained devotion and effort to understand and bring to birth in family life and relationships a certain pattern of life.

The matter can be put into a single sentence: A Christian home is one in which the ideals for living found in the life and teachings of Jesus Christ are accepted, exalted, and exemplified. Jesus Christ is the center of the Christian home. The things he stood for, his estimates of life, of other people, of one's duty toward them, of the supremacy of love as the ultimate power in life—these are woven into the fabric of a Christian home. We need to understand both their claim on us and their promise for us, if they are to guide in our witness.

The Christian estimate of life itself sets the stage for all else. Life is not a private possession to take lightly, to treat as we please and to use by whatever rules we may desire. Life is a gift from God himself, brought to us through our ancestors and the long tradition of which we are a part. Life therefore is a sacred trust, something given to us in faith by men of faith before us. We have not earned it any more than we have asked for it; yet it is the thread on which are strung all of our being and days. It is colored with the experience of yesterday, vibrant with the meaning of the relationships of today, and pregnant with possibilities for the unfolding future. Underlying it, infused through it, investing it with purpose and meaning, is the will of God—the Creator, Sustainer and Redeemer of life.

If this be the correct estimate of life, as the Christian faith maintains, then life is no bauble to be enjoyed for a moment, no fitful dream that is dissolved in death. It is a major moral trust, and the way a person lives it is the true measure of his worth.

Add to this estimate of life the further estimate that people possessed of the Christian faith place upon other people. All persons are creatures of God, even as we faithfully trust we are. Different as we may be in color, nationality, creed, possessions, and in many other ways, we are one in this respect: We are creatures of God, and we ought to live together as brothers one of another. The Christian faith does not let us off with the easy notation that we are like each other; it drives home the profound spiritual and ethical truth that we ought to love one another. This, of course, deepens the requirement of sensitivity almost beyond bearing, and yet it must be attempted. It means that Christian people will try to be completely sensitive and responsive to the personality, the needs and the relationships of others. It means that they will do everything in their power to give every person both the right and the encouragement to bring to full fruit the divinely implanted abilities of his own life.

Actually, the best way to describe the human meaning of a Christian home is to say that it is a relationship which seeks to be a living embodiment of the love of God. For two thousand years we have been saying that "God is love," and in this insistence we have indicated the true foundation of all that we do in the name of our Christian faith.

Love begins with the honest recognition of our interdependence with other people. Our life is a part of theirs— theirs a part of ours. No man has ever been or ever will be self-sufficient. "No man is an island, entire of itself!" We need each other and are needed by each other. And he who denies this by word or in life sins against the deepest and truest thing about him and against all who are intertwined with him in the "bundle of life." Love begins, then, with an honest and responsible recognition of this interdependence among people.

Christian love does not accept this interdependence grudgingly, but joyously as an open door to the greatest good known to us. Some stop short at this point and ask to be excused from further effort. We seem to resent, upon occasion, the fact that our lives are inseparably related to others; we both resent it and fight against it. A young mother, swamped with three small children, once said that she found herself resenting them because they took so much of her time, energy, and thought that she had all but ceased to be a person in her own right. Unconsciously she found herself fighting the deepest currents in her own life—the will of God which through her interdependence with her family was creating of her a new and richer person.

It is a tragic mistake to set ourselves up in opposition to those with whom our lives are deeply related. The tragedy is not exhausted in the hurt we do another; it includes the hurt we do ourselves as well. The more we hurt another the worse we wound ourselves—this is the negative side of the law of love. We do not and cannot find anything like the fulfillment of our own life either in isolation from others or at the expense of others. We cannot purchase happiness for ourselves at a price to be paid by another—not so long as God reigns in the life of man.

Love—the kind of love that undergirds the Christian witness in family and home—is willingness to share the best that we have and all that we have without the thought of restraint or reward. Not many parents reason as did one tired, anxious, half-defeated mother, "Children just don't pay. They cost all the time. I get tired of paying the bills." Yet, had anyone tried to take her two little girls from her she would have fought them from Dan to Beersheba! In one sense she was giving her life for them, but in a deeper sense she was finding her life in the process of giving it to them, sharing it with them. When this was explained to her in the context of the New Testament word: "He that findeth his life shall lose it; and he that loseth his life for my sake shall find it" (Matthew 10:39) she said: "That is the first time I have ever understood that verse—or myself."

Love, then, is the open and honest recognition and joyful acceptance of the fact that we are members one of another; that the greatest possible good lies in it; that love is a way of life that literally gives common relationships new meaning, the divine meaning implanted in all by the God of all.

One of the most wonderful descriptions of the true relationships between the home and altar came from the pen of a late editor of *The New York Times* when he wrote, "A dining room table with children's eager, hungry faces around it, ceases to be a mere dining room table, and becomes an altar." When I recall our parental home with eight children clustered around that table, I cannot help thinking it one of the busiest, happiest altars in all Christendom!

Some twenty years ago a group of Christian leaders from various parts of the world gathered in Madras, India, to consider the meaning of the Christian way of life in the modern world. Among other things they tried to describe the essential qualities of a Christian home anywhere and everywhere in the world. Here are some of their answers: A Christian home is a community, a place of well-being, a haven of peace, a school, a wonderful fellowship, a refuge, a place of vision where people learn the meaning of common life.

While the Christian home ideally at least is all of these, it is one thing more: a source of strength sufficient for the hardest work under the most difficult trials of life. That is why I tell the couples who come to me for counseling before marriage, that the home is no "fairweather" arrangement to be entered into when things are going well and to be deserted when the going gets difficult. We do not enlist in the Christian home for a limited period of service: we enlist in it for life if ever we are to serve it in spirit and in truth.

I tell them—with what success I have no way of knowing —that the love which brings them to the altar will, if properly nurtured, sustain them throughout a lifetime of the most difficult experiences imaginable. In their love, they can find the divine resources they need for the management of whatever they must face. A Christian home is sheer spiritual strength; it cannot be broken from assaults from without, but it can be betrayed and surrendered from within.

And I remind them that they can help each other more,

and hurt each other worse, in marriage and the home than in any other relationship they will ever have. Whenever they enter into the life of love and responsible relationships which we have in the home, they are inside each other's guard; they are completely vulnerable to what each other may say or do. Their home will last as long as their love will last; if their love should disappear, there will be no substance or meaning to the home.

III

If we want the Christian way of life to permeate every family and home, our duty is clear. We must take seriously the idea of a Christian home and begin to make it come alive in our own home. We will accept the sacredness of the relationship we have in the home. The home will become a kind of sanctuary where we have our deepest dealings, not alone with each other, but with God.

To the extent that we are willing and able to do this we shall be building a Christian home. We shall have a standard, a goal for our efforts. We shall not simply mill around, led this way and that by whim and emotion, hoping somehow to wake up with a stable, creative Christian home. Rather, through our dedication to the ideal and our determination to achieve it as best we can, our homes will take on Christian character and find Christian strength. To the extent that we are able to do this, we shall be fitting ourselves and our children for the great issues of the day in which we live.

Mrs. David Jones, whose husband was for many years the distinguished president of Bennett College in Greensboro, North Carolina, once put all this in vivid words, "If children are to love people, love peace, work together with others harmoniously, they stand a better chance if they come from homes where there is love, security, and mutual sharing."

Living as we do in a world that is dying for lack of these very qualities, we cannot help wondering what chance we have of turning the tide. Our one and only source of confidence that this can be done can be put quite simply: The universe is on our side in the effort. The God of all is the God of love. Love is the most powerful force on earth. We can find our way in the love of God. As we find our way in it, we will know a power and a purpose that this world can neither give nor take away.

Racial Relations

I

PEARL BUCK'S grim prediction that the battle lines of
World War III would be the color lines of the world
seems to be borne out by events. Easily the most disturbing
and potentially far-reaching conflicts in the world today are
across some "color line" or other. The cold war between
communism and democracy pales into insignificance when
laid alongside the conflicts both hot and cold that are either
in being or in prospect over the issues of "color." The efforts
of the white race to continue to hold the fruits of domination
are being both challenged and defeated everywhere. The policy
of colonialism is as dead as the dodo bird. Yet the prejudices
and conventions associated with that policy linger on.

The Christian way of life in racial relations must find
expression above the roar of this world-wide battle. And,
let it be said to the credit of the Christian churches, they are
trying to do just that—at least in their top-level, policy-
making meetings. But high-sounding resolutions that ring
so grandly in the assemblies of the World Council, or on the
floor of general meetings of the larger denominations, are
frequently strangled at once by hard prejudices in many local
churches. And the hands used for strangling are pious plati-

tudes and determined prejudices. It is a terrifying thing to face the plain fact that the best we know is prostituted to the worst we feel over the issue of the color line.

But progress has been made and, in spite of growing difficulties, it must be continued. Every church in Christendom is aroused over racial problems and the day of hiding from them is clearly over. This is not to say that a period of peaceful solution is at hand, but we may take courage from the fact that the need for expressing the Christian way of life in racial matters is now accepted by all churches.

II

As one illustration, the General Conference of The Methodist Church has expressed itself concerning race both in resolutions and legislation. The Episcopal Address that opened the General Conference in 1956 included this significant statement.

> In our world, our nation, and our church, however, racial discrimination and segregation do exist. As sincere followers of our Lord it is our business to help free our world and our nation from these evils. But it is more immediately our imperative duty to confess our failure to achieve God's will in Methodism and then resolutely to set about achieving a Christian brotherhood in the church that will be free from racial discrimination and segregation. . . .

In a resolution this same body added:

> There must be no place in The Methodist Church for racial discrimination or enforced segregation. Recognizing that we have not attained this goal, yet rejoicing in the progress made, we recommend that discrimination or segregation by any method or

practice, whether by conference structure or otherwise, in The Methodist Church be abolished with reasonable speed. The growing spirit of brotherhood throughout the church strengthens our confidence that, under the leadership of the Holy Spirit, we will continue to go forward.

The Church Woman, the official publication of the United Church Women in this country, carried in its issue of May, 1957, a summary of the positions of the seventeen major Protestant churches on the matter of segregation in the public schools. In every case there is complete agreement on the basic approach to this and other problems of race relations. The unity of thought of Christian groups regarding race is further borne out by the report of the Christian Life Commission of the Southern Baptist Convention in 1957. A portion of that report reads:

> We appeal to our Baptist brethren, white and Negro, and to other Christian friends, to give careful consideration to the following statement of principles, setting forth, we believe, the truth of the Bible and offered in the spirit of good will and Christian love:
>
> 1. God created man in his own image. Therefore, every man possesses infinite worth and should be treated with respect as a person.
>
> 2. Christ died for all men. Therefore, the Christian view of man, every man, must reflect the spirit of the cross.
>
> 3. God is no respector of persons. Therefore, prejudice against persons or mistreatment of persons on the grounds of race is contrary to the will of God.
>
> 4. Christ said, "Thou shalt love thy neighbor as thyself." Therefore, Christians are obligated to manifest active goodwill toward all people and to help them to achieve their fullest potentialities as persons.
>
> 5. Christian love, as exemplified by Christ, is the

supreme law for all human relations. Therefore, Christians have the assurance that such love,
conscientiously practiced, will resolve tensions and
bring harmony and good will in race relations.

6. All true Christians are brothers in Christ and
children of God. Therefore, they are obligated to
cultivate prayerful concern for one another and to
show confidence in one another.

7. Every person is accountable to God. Therefore,
the right of individual opinion, tested by the teachings
of Christ, and of freedom to express it, always in the
spirit of Christian love, should be granted to all and
respected by all.

In accordance with these principles of our Christian
faith, and as free citizens, this Commission protests
the violence in all its ugly forms that is being used
against the Negro people in the current segregation
issue or at any other time. In recognition of the
Negro's rights as a citizen of these United States,
we call upon the law enforcement agencies of local,
state, and national governments to protect him, irre-
spective of his position or culture, from lawless attacks on his person or property.

III

The World Council of Churches has been equally clear
and firm in its approach to the need for and meaning of the
Christian witness in racial relations.

When the World Council speaks on these problems it
does so with a clear consciousness that they have been before
the churches of the world with increasing intensity over the
last half century. This is particularly true of the churches of
the United States, Asia, and Africa. Thanks to the influence
of liberalism and the social gospel, churches in the United
States were confronted more than fifty years ago with the
sin of the color line within themselves as well as in society.

We in the churches were forced to stand up and make answer for our sins on this matter. We were aided and spurred by a rising concern for justice throughout our country which manifests itself in many ways.

The problems of racial relations have been explored by scientific studies as well as exposed by novels, dramas, and motion pictures. Both young and old alike are well acquainted with them. That explains why the position taken by the World Council of Churches in the two assemblies held to date adds little, if anything, to those already taken by every major church in this country. To say this is not to minimize the importance of what the World Council says. It is both necessary and important for the World Council to raise a banner in this area of race relations as well as in other areas to which the Christian conscience will rally its forces for war against injustice in every form. The Second Assembly of the World Council meeting in Evanston said three important things on this matter, and they apply to each church and each churchman.

First, it outlined the Christian approach to the problems of race; second, it confronted the churches with certain duties; third, it asked all confessing Christians to re-examine their position as churchmen as well as a church.

The World Council began, as we must begin, with the plain fact that the problems of race are world-wide in scope and aggravate every other problem—political, economic, or social—that we must face. The political problems of Asia and Africa can not be discussed apart from the racial problem.

This, then, is not a problem for a few of us; it belongs to all men. It is a world problem in the exact sense that it has come, or at any moment may come, to flaming focus anywhere on earth. It is not the creation of the southern states in the United States, or of Harlem in New York City, or of the

South Side in Chicago. If by some magic we could clear up the trouble in these areas, racism would continue in virulent form in a dozen other places on the surface of the earth.

The World Council raises the question as to whether or not the Christian approach to these problems is different from that of a non-Christian. The answer is in the affirmative:

> It is our Christian belief that our Lord is concerned for all just hopes of men but in Himself He offers the hope that transcends them all. The Bible teaches us that God is the Sovereign Creator of all men, and by Him they are sustained and have their being. When He made the world, He saw that it was good. But man by his sin—by his disobedience and pride and the lifting of his arm against his brother—has filled it with division and distrust.
>
> What is the Christian hope in this disunity? It is Jesus Christ, who revealed God as Father and who died for all men, reconciling them to God and to each other by His Cross. From every race and nation a new people of God is created, in which the power of the Spirit overcomes racial pride and fear. So far from being without hope or purpose, God's people now as new creatures are co-workers with Him, and are filled with joy, and assured His final victory.
>
> So to us is given the gift of sharing in and working for the Kingdom even now. Assured that the final victory is Christ's, we can work actively, continually repentant and continually forgiven, for that reconciliation which we believe to be God's will.
>
> This is the calling of the Church with regard to race, to witness within itself to the Kingship of Christ and the unity of His people, in Him transcending all diversity. Jesus Christ in His Incarnation and redemptive action restores this unity which from the beginning was God's design.[1]

---

[1] W. A. Visser 't Hooft (ed.), *The Evanston Report* (New York, Harper & Bros., 1955), pages 152-3. Used by permission.

In the fulfillment of this task, the World Council asked churches and churchmen to address themselves to certain duties. While these are general enough to sharpen up our Christian responsibility on all social problems, they have special relevance on the problems of racial relations. (1) We must be willing "to obey and to proclaim the word of judgment." (2) We must be willing "to repent and to call to repentance." (3) We must be willing to challenge the conscience of society both by what we believe and by what we are as Christians and as the Christian church.

These apparently placid statements explode with revolutionary violence when we use them in interpreting our responsibility on matters of race.

Christians are called to obey as well as to proclaim the judgment of God, who made us one and in whose holy sight all divisions and strife are sinful. We are called to repent of the strife in our own fellowship and to call to repentance men, races, and nations that struggle against each other. We are called to renounce strife and conflict among ourselves as sinful, and to persuade other men to do likewise. We are called upon to reject racial or ethnic fears and prejudices as neither necessary nor good, and to accept them as being evil because they separate man and obscure God's will for man. We are called upon to reject racial segregation in all forms as an outgrowth of such fears.

Actually, if we want to go to the root of this matter of racial injustice, we shall find it in our own sinfulness. And if we want to bear the Christian witness against the evil, we begin not by an assault upon someone else but by an act of profound soul-searching within ourselves.

Then, and only then, is the church ready to challenge the conscience of society. For we shall need insight, wisdom, courage, and, if possible, a deep sense of fellowship with one another and with God as we confront the "kings" of our time with the word, "Thou art the man!"

The duty of issuing this challenge is not limited to the preacher in the pulpit; it would be wholly ineffectual if that were true. It rests upon the church—minister and layman alike.

In challenging the conscience of society, the church must be ready to understand and extend support to the adventurous ones among us who look for new ways out of the darkness of this problem. We can neither expect nor ask of all in our fellowship close conformity to law and slavish obedience to custom when we are searching desperately for a way out of profound confusion and desperate conflict. We must expect adventurous spirits among us to come forward with proposals, experiments, and deeds that will startle, if not shock, us. When that occurs, we will want to be sympathetic in our understanding and patient in our judgment even when we are forced to differ with the proposals advanced.

As if to illustrate the realism of its determination to do this, the World Council raises a matter for consideration which is all but taboo in any discussion of racial problems by churchmen or anyone else in this country, namely, intermarriage. As a matter of fact, intermarriage is a very small problem in point of view of the number of times its must be confronted in concrete form. Yet it is raised as a dark and sinister menace with great frequency in many discussions of race. To my knowledge, the World Council is the first major body of churches and churchmen ever to comment on any phase of the matter in an official utterance. Certainly no church in the United States has done so as yet.

The World Council raises the matter not in order to advocate intermarriage, or to persuade people to expect it, but as an example of legal discrimination based on race and in order (1) to remove false religious reasons frequently involved in the discussion of these discriminations and (2) to chart a path for churches to follow when confronted by the problem in concrete form:

> The Church of Christ cannot approve of any law which discriminates on grounds of race, which restricts the opportunity of any person to acquire education to prepare himself for his vocation, to procure or to practise employment in his vocation, or in any other way curtails his exercise of the full rights and responsibilities of citizenship and of sharing in the responsibilities and duties of government. While it can find in the Bible no clear justification or condemnation of intermarriage, but only a discussion of the duties of the faithful in marriage with partners of other religions, it cannot approve any law against racial or ethnic intermarriage, for Christian marriage involves primarily a union of two individuals before God which goes beyond the jurisdiction of the state or of culture.
>
> A minister of the Church should advise young people, when preparing them for the grave responsibilities of intermarriage, both of the potential richness of such marriages and of the painful consequences in some situations, which consequences are often caused by the hardness of men's hearts and by cultural differences. There is no evidence that the children of such marriages are inherently inferior, and any treatment of them as such should be condemned.[2]

The World Council urges the kind of adventuring now going on all over the United States in the development of interracial churches where they best serve the needs of the community. Many such churches have already come into existence, particularly in large cities. Many more will cer-

[2] *Ibid.,* pages 156-7. Used by permission.

tainly develop. Here again the entire church is asked to
understand the situation as Christians and to support those
of our fellowship who believe that this represents the right
answer. We are asked to hold in close fellowship those who
for conscience' sake have not hesitated in the past, and do
not hesitate now, to challenge any law, custom, or convention
which impedes the unfolding will of God for the community
of the human family:

> We are concerned here with our hopes for the
> peace and unity of all mankind, but what greater hope
> there would be if only our Christian unity were
> achieved, a unity transcending the ethnic and racial
> difference of all believers. That is our urgent and
> immediate task; when it is accomplished how great
> the further contribution that we might make.[3]

IV

The fact of discrimination and segregation on racial lines in
our common life has translated itself into the law and
administrative structure of most churches. As most persons
know, in the structure of The Methodist Church in the
United States are five geographical divisions and one racial
division called "jurisdictions." Although there is considerable
desire in the church to remove the jurisdiction based on race,
the problem of how this can best be done has been aggravating
the church since union in 1939. But one thing is clear: So
long as any church tolerates a separate grouping based on race,
it is a segregated church.

There may be those among us who find any effort to end
racial segregation and discrimination a scandal to their
prejudices, and who wonder where they can go to escape it.

---

[3] *Ibid.*, page 158. Used by permission.

There is only one thing to say to those who feel this way: There is no place to hide from it any longer.

There is not a single church in the World Council or in the National Council of Churches that is not committed along every line already mentioned. If we are able to find a church that will cater to our racial prejudices, then write it down for a fact that that church is breaking faith with the witness of the Christian gospel and is completely out of step with both Catholic and Protestant traditions the world over. Quite literally, then, there is no place to hide from the onrushing day when the Christian fellowship, like Isaiah's house of prayer, will be "for all peoples."

Let us be quite clear on the exact nature of the choice before us: We can delay the coming of that day, though we cannot prevent it; or we can work for it and speed its coming.

Not many of us honestly want to hide from that day. Rather, let us face it as a door to the Kingdom opened by the Lord of history. We have to work with patience, tolerance, and good will at the thousand and one hard problems and tasks that must be performed by churchmen and churches as we prepare for entrance.

8

Economic Relations

I

A SIGNIFICANT development in the Christian tradition over the last century was the emergence of a strong and clearly articulated social conscience. Catholic and Protestant traditions alike engaged in this process, and it is still in its early stages. Under the strong leadership of Leo XIII the continuing and expanding concern of the Roman Catholic Church for the many problems that emerge in the field of economic relations was begun and has been continued. Heroic figures like Walter Rauschenbusch and many others in the United States and England, and on the continents of Europe, Asia, and Africa have performed a similar service in the Protestant tradition.

As a result of these beginnings and continued efforts, every major church in Christendom has a "social creed" or some statement which serves in its stead. It is no longer possible for the Christian Church to bear its witness without articulating itself in terms of the social and economic relations of mankind. The Federal Council of Churches and its successor organization, the National Council of Churches, have sponsored a series of representative conferences to deal with the church and economic life. As the result of these efforts, there has been a constant stream of scholarly publications dealing with various facets of this problem. The church is alert, informed, and determined to bear its witness in this area.

When the World Council of Churches meets in General Assembly, whether in Amsterdam, Evanston, or Ceylon, the great and grave problems in economic relations are certain to receive careful attention. The delegates to these conferences may represent different churches and be motivated by different theological beliefs, but they sit down with one accord before such problems and seek to discover the Christian way to meet the issues found in that area.

The doubts and criticism which have been raised about the development of the churches' concern in this area revolve around one or more questions. By what authority does the Church concern herself with these problems? To what end does the Christian witness seek to move thought and life in them?

In reply to the first we might content ourselves by saying that we are clothed in the authority of the living God, the Creator, Sustainer, and Redeemer of the world who seeks today as of old the welfare of all his children. God spoke to Moses saying, "Come now therefore, and I will send thee unto Pharaoh, that thou mayest bring forth my people the children of Israel out of Egypt." (Exodus 3:10.) God spoke to Israel through Amos saying, "Let judgment run down as waters, and righteousness as a mighty stream." (Amos 5:24.) God spoke to Judah through Isaiah asking, "What mean ye that ye beat my people to pieces, and grind the faces of the poor?" (Isaiah 3:15.) The God of the probing ethical conscience of ancient Israel and the recent past is seeking to speak to the troubled heart and life of our world today through churchmen and churches.

We address ourselves to our task, not by permission of

men but by the commission of God—the God whom we
meet in transcendent glory in the New Testament. The God
we worship seeks the welfare of all his children, even as a
shepherd searches for one lost sheep or a father for one lost
son. His nature is love, for he "so loved the world that he gave
his only begotten Son, that whosoever believeth in him should
not perish, but have everlasting life." (John 3:16.) Jesus
Christ commissioned his followers to go to the ends of the
earth as witnesses to all men.

Christians concern themselves with these problems by the
authority of the evolving ethical conscience of the Christian
tradition through nearly two thousand years of history.
Without claiming for one moment that all has been well
with the church through the centuries, the plain fact remains
that she has rendered an incalculable contribution to human
welfare and well-being, both in the living of life here and in
anticipation of the life to come. Schools, hospitals, asylums,
orphanages, and churches—these are some of the creatures
of the maturing ethical conscience of the Christian faith.
Practice after practice—slavery, infanticide, racism, nationalism, and war—has been brought before the bar of Christian
judgment and pronounced evil. Whenever, wherever, and
for whatever reason the health of the bodies, minds, and
spirits of men is endangered either by injustice, misunderstanding, or fratricidal conflict, there Christians have not
only a clear duty but also an unassailable mandate to be
present, and to be present as ministers of the living God.

It is against this background that the church sums up her
right to be heard in the area of economic relations in the most
uncompromising manner. She has a right to be heard because
of the plain fact that the whole range of life belongs to God.
Nothing human is alien to him, nor can it be to the church
which seeks to serve him. Gone is the day when churchmen

would permit themselves to be either shoved unceremoniously or bowed politely out of any area where human values, human relationships, and human lives are at stake. The church is involved all along the line in every major economic problem, because the church is composed of men and women in the management, labor, and consumer groups. Whatever affects them—any of them—affects the church, and the church has the right and the duty to take serious cognizance of the situation. Whoever argues otherwise would say, in effect, that a hole in the hull of a sinking ship is the concern of the captain and the crew but not of the passengers!

The church concerns herself with these problems because she is needed there. She has a contribution to make apart from which they cannot be solved.

II

Yet the problems which confront us in the area of industrial relations alone, to select one phase of economic relations, are complex enough to "make cowards of us all."

In his *Study of History,* Professor Arnold Toynbee says that "industrialism" and "democracy" are the two distinctive characteristics of modern civilization. Both are in grave trouble just now, and it is an open question whether either can survive. As a matter of fact, Dr. Toynbee argues that the basic conflict in the modern world is between industrialism on the one hand and democracy on the other.

The case as he develops it proceeds something like this: The needs of modern industry created huge pools of workers in cities. In its early days, industry was the personal property of one man or a few men at most. It was essentially feudal in its pattern of power and responsibility. Owners were laws unto themselves in policies of purchase and sale of goods, as well as in the hours, conditions, and wages of labor. Understandably, the ferment of democracy, which in two centuries had overthrown the doctrine of the divine right of kings and the absolute monarchies of Europe, has placed the right of franchise in the hands of citizens. Democracy has also produced movements for greater freedom, dignity, and security among workingmen. It is difficult to see how the leaven of democracy could have been prevented from working in the field of industry.

The logic of democracy is inexorable. Each man is the bearer of infinite worth because he is the child of God. Each man is entitled to a voice in the determination of the laws under which he lives and the selection of the government which is to administer the laws. Each man is entitled to a voice in the determination of the policies, the life, and the structure of the industry on which he is dependent for his livelihood. Until and unless we can compartmentalize ideas, and thus confine the meaning of democracy to the area of citizenship, it will keep right on challenging any and every allocation of power that is beyond the reach of the persons who are affected by the use of that power.

In these latter days, both industry and democracy have been and are being challenged by various forms of fascism and communism which, if successful, will alter them beyond recognition. So the problems we face in the field are all tangled up with history, politics, and international events and policies. Emerging from the many problems in detail are certain problems in principle—and these are now under discussion and dispute. They might be phrased this way: (1) the democratizing of power; (2) social stability through social change; and (3) personal and group freedom in community. To one who challenges our right to consider problems like these in the field of industry, we say that the

Christian faith is prepared to make a contribution to the solution of these problems. And that contribution lies in both the end to be sought and the reason why we seek it.

III

In answer to the query, "To what end do you seek to move our common thought and life in these matters?" we must say, at the risk of triteness, "Toward the kingdom of God." That is the goal, the end, the ultimate purpose of the Christian Church, because it is the ultimate aim of the will of God as found in Jesus Christ. That is the banner under which the Christian Church enters this and every other area of human conflict. Justice, security, peace, and community—the importance of these nearer goals will not be minimized. Yet the most certain way for the Christian faith to minimize them is to wrench them out of the context from which they derive their final validation, i.e., the concept of the kingdom of God. We do not dishonor them by putting the kingdom of God first; rather we thereby supply the frame of reference in which they find the widest possible scope of meaning.

Separate them from the idea of the kingdom of God and they become prudential instruments for the removal of conflict without any affirmative convictions about the nature of the life that will result. The question "Why seek justice?" could be answered, "To remove conflict and injustice." But a persistent skeptic will want to know, "Why remove conflict and injustice?" Without a further affirmative notion as to what life ought to be like, there is no real answer to that. With the idea of the kingdom of God in mind, a final answer can be given.

While we are not able to produce a set of blueprints for realizing the kingdom of God in human life, we may make certain general statements about its nature that will indicate its relevance to our life and history.

First, as God's kingdom, it is one in which his will is acknowledged and obeyed. Nor are we wholly in the dark as to what his will is. The beliefs outlined in the opening section of this book have won their way to general acceptance in the Christian tradition. With them in mind, it is easy to understand William Temple's very realistic conclusion: "The kingdom of God is the sovereignty of love, and the subordination of power to love is the principle of that kingdom." To believe in love as the true order of reality, to feel its power toward oneness, is to live in the kingdom of God.

A second implication of the kingdom of God is this: it reminds us that all our plans, policies, institutions, and creations must finally square with the fact of God or perish. History is not morally neutral. The kingdom of God is both within us and within history as guide and judge. The kingdom of God is not a "far-off day toward which the whole creation moves"; it is a reality—in part actual, in part potential—in human life and history. Hence, the Christian faith insists that every one of us must constantly answer this question: "Does this proposal, practice, or institution square with the meaning of the kingdom of God?" This is the only ultimately important question, and it is also the most immediately relevant question.

It adds up to this: the Christian faith insists that what we do we ought to do for God's sake and for the sake of his kingdom. The Christian faith is not primarily concerned with the preservation of democracy, the American way of life, free enterprise, capitalism—even laissez-faire capitalism —unionism, the white race, the Protestant or the Catholic Church. Instead, the Christian faith is, or ought to be, characterized by humble devotion to the petition: "Thy

kingdom come. Thy will be done in earth, as it is in heaven."
And if, in making actual that will of God, even cherished
national cultural or social conventions and practices need
to be altered, if not abandoned, so be it; let his will be done.

Study the notion of the kingdom of God for a moment
and we see two great centers of confidence emerging from
it: God can be depended upon; and man, under God, can be
depended upon. We are not trying to build bricks without
straw when we try to build the kingdom of God with and of
men neither better nor wiser than we are. There is an
essential core of dependability and reliability about man, the
child of God, and upon this we can and must rely. Indeed, no
new answer is possible to the problems we face if we act
on any other assumption. On any other assumption—democracy is a mockery, community is a fool's paradise, and a
world of justice, peace, and security is a myth.

Believing as we do in God, in the activity of God in life and
history, and in man, under God, we are able to say without
hesitation that the end we seek is the fuller discovery and
more perfect realization of the kingdom of God in our
common life and history. We approach the problems of
industry, race, denominations, and nations with this and
only this end in view. To the kingdom of God and it alone
can be given our supreme loyalty. Christians are not primarily
concerned to make modern industrialism or capitalism or
socialism or labor unionism work. Our primary aim is to bring
this entire troubled area in the life of mankind before the
judgment bar of the kingdom of God. To the extent that we
are able honestly and humbly to do this we will have made a
supreme effort to separate the better from the worse in each
and to preserve the better. But, let it be known, the judgments
"better and worse" derive from the nature and reality of
the kingdom of God and not from any other standard.

To the extent that we are able to let the logic of the Christian faith control us, we shall be neither surprised nor appalled at the certainty that deep-lying changes in our social order must be consciously and persistently sought in order that the kingdom of God may come. We shall confront the confusion of our times confident that it can be brought to a stable order if we are able to discover in its disorder the meaning of the kingdom of God.

IV

Jesus came teaching and preaching and living these convictions: (1) God is the supreme fact in life and the world. (2) All men are his children. (3) Life is a divine trust and all living is a dealing with God. Thus he unfurled the banner under which we try to march. For these convictions are not so much ideas to be weighed as journeys to be taken. As we take them we shall find ourselves in possession of a far different view of life and history than we now have. And, what is immeasurably more difficult, we shall find ourselves under the compulsion to be instruments of the redemptive will of God as he seeks to transform the world from what it is to what it ought to be.

No one knew better than Jesus that these convictions prefigured the complete transformation of life and history. To take them seriously is to become a new creature in Christ. Difficult as it is to live with them, we are finding life without them literally impossible. We are learning the hard way that unless life is treated as a divine trust the human situation rapidly becomes intolerable. Treat other persons, or races, or nations as means to our end, as instruments in purposes that serve our own welfare, and we, to the extent that we are successful, have made revolution inevitable. Yet the illusions nourished by power, wealth, and position continue to darken our perception of this fact. Military power is such an impressive fact that in a day of confusion or uncertainty men turn to it as a kind of guarantor of security. We read the judgment of a military analyst: "We are the masters of our fate." We hear the judgment of a news commentator on world affairs: "History is what men make it. If we do not choose to get out and make it what we want, at whatever cost, it is going to be made for us by other men, who are willing to work at it."

Such counsels are more than futile; they are fatal. To say that history is what we make it is to utter a most dangerous half-truth. The full and true version is this: History is what God permits us to make it. It is the scene of our dealing with God and his dealing with us. It is true that we are free to try to build any kind of social order we choose; but the validity of our plan and the permanence of our building are determined by a power entirely beyond our control. James Anthony Froude, after a lifetime spent in the study of history, bears this impressive witness: "One lesson and only one, history may be said to repeat with distinctiveness: that the world is built somehow on moral foundations; that in the long run it is well with the good; in the long run it is ill with the wicked."

Almost from the beginning of the Christian tradition, the church has sensed the costliness of such convictions. The transformation of life and history, plainly implicit in them, could not be accomplished by verbal proclamation of them; they had to "come alive," to become incarnate in the lives of men and in history, before they could become the way of salvation. Our Lord made it clear that one could know the vocabulary of religion, say, "Lord, Lord," and yet not know or be known by its transforming power. Looking back upon

the faith of Jesus as he went among his fellow men and on
the fate they meted out to him, Paul counseled his hearers
to remember, "Ye are bought with a price." The cross became
the symbol of the fate of Jesus and of the price which any
man who follows him must be prepared to pay. Whether the
gospel of salvation spreads slowly or fast, every inch of
advance is "bought with a price"—that is the unqualified
testimony of nineteen hundred years of Christian history.

V

There are those who would dismiss the social creeds of the
several churches as "minority reports" in the life of the
church. There is a sense in which this is true. Although
written and adopted by a representative assembly of churchmen, composed in part of laity as well as clergy, all such
assemblies are minorities so far as the general public is
concerned. The same is true of Congress, the Supreme Court,
and the assemblies of the World Council of Churches.

But there is a far deeper sense in which this is a minority
report. The Christian church has always been a minority
group within the life of the world. Even if every confessing
Christian churchman the world over were to subscribe gladly
to the social creed of his church, it would still be a minority
report. But the fact should not terrify us. We should face it
with the words Lord Passmore wrote in his review of the
Letters of Beatrice and Sidney Webb, two of the outstanding
students of social and labor problems of our times: "They
signed many minority reports which became majority
actions."

Political Relations

I

CHRISTIANS must frame their witness in terms of the political forms and problems in which they find themselves.

I believe in the Christian religion as the true view of life and in democracy as the form of society in which the Christian view can best mature. I am concerned, therefore, to indicate those points at which Christianity can contribute something essential to the survival of democracy. For I am convinced that the paramount political problem before us today is this: *Can democracy survive?*

This leads to further questions: Can Christianity help democracy meet the challenge of skepticism as to the validity of the democratic ideal? Can Christianity furnish the fertile soil of positive faith in man, in history, and in the future which is essential to the survival of man's confidence in democracy? Can Christianity help keep democracy from becoming a dogma, a static entity and help keep it facing forward, growing in terms of new problems? Can Christianity lift democracy above the provincialism of nationalism and the barbarism of imperialism, thus enabling it to be the champion of human rights wherever they are imperiled?

These serious questions deserve more time and much more wisdom than we can hope to bring to bear upon them, but they are too momentous to ignore. A wrong answer is better than no answer, since it manifests an awareness of the importance of the question and a determination to attempt an answer to it.

The basic question to be faced can be stated in simple terms: Are men capable of democracy? We are not asking whether we want democracy or whether we are willing to work for it. We are raising the much deeper question as to whether there is any use even trying to achieve it. We shall find that men have faced uncertainty on this basic problem wherever they have tried to think their way into the meaning of democracy.

A good definition of democracy is Abraham Lincoln's famous phrase, a "government of the people, by the people, for the people." But this conception is widely challenged both in theory and practice. That gifted snob, Henry Adams, in his *Degradation of the Democratic Dogma*,[1] wrote, "Democracy is an infinite mass of conflicting minds and of conflicting interests which . . . becomes resolved into . . . a vapor, which loses in collective intellectual energy in proportion to the perfection of its expansion." This is another way of saying that the farther you spread democracy, the less actual interest in it and the less understanding of it there is among people in general. A militant minority can agitate for and finally win democratic rights for the majority, but the majority will let them slip through negligent fingers. Perhaps this prompted Thomas Carlyle to say, "Democracy is a plurality of blockheads."

Lincoln's conception of democracy has had hard sledding in history. To begin with, it has seldom been tried, and when

---

[1] The Macmillan Co., New York. 1920, page 109. Used by permission.

it has, the results have not been encouraging. Democracy in Periclean Greece lived with a measure of effectiveness for one hundred years, but it weakened and finally fell. It failed because it was unable to manage the vices that arose within it. It was irremediably weakened by internal enemies before it succumbed to external ones.

Unfortunately, democracy seems to be in a similar predicament today. After having been in operation to some extent in the Western World for several hundred years, it is now fighting for its very life against doubts and vices within and deadly foes without. The question persists: Why is it that democracy has so much trouble if it is based upon a true appraisal of human capacities? One of the few philosopher-statesmen of our day, Professor T. V. Smith, once laid bare the heart of the democratic problem with this penetrating observation: "That men will live for private gain we know; that they will die for public ends we know, but whether average men in the continuous long run will work efficiently for public ends we do not know." Nor is Dr. Smith alone in this doubt. Some of the most disciplined minds the human race has ever produced would question whether we can count on the average man's willingness to do those things that are essential to democracy.

Plato and a host of other eminent thinkers had no faith at all in the possibility of building an enduring, democratic society. For Plato, democracy is always and inevitably corrupted by human greed and pride. The reason is simple: *Democracy gives the individual more freedom than he can manage.* Instead of asking "What is the public good?" he asks "What do I want?" He sets himself up as a determiner of what he wants and is sublimely unconcerned about the wants of others. When conflict arises between his desires and the desires of others, as it inevitably does, each individual is willing to usurp the rights of others in order to secure his own. He will utilize the freedom democracy gives him to gratify his own selfish and uncriticized desires. He will regard it as an opportunity to exploit his own undisciplined passions at the expense of other people and their freedom.

Thus democracy will break up as the result of internal changes. Many men see one man gain an increasing amount of power. Wanting to share in its fruits, they will gravitate to him, let him serve as their protector, and pay the price. He will promise them bread and circuses or anything else that they appear to want, if they will assign him their right to make the decisions by which they are to live. Most people will do just that, the critics of democracy contend. When democracy is tried in this fashion, they contend, it moves from a short-lived experience of individual freedom to a long-lived experience of tyranny.

II

Standing firmly on the foundation of our faith in God and man, and our hard-won experience in trying to articulate the Christian witness over nearly two thousand years, Christians continue to believe that man is capable of living in a responsible way in a democratic society. Thus we are called to face with confidence the major spiritual problems of democracy—pride, greed, prejudices, and ignorance. We do this knowing that these problems will not be solved by overthrowing political or military powers that may challenge us as a democratic society at any given moment, however dangerous the challenge may be. No matter how many external enemies we may conquer, the basic internal problems will persist. Unless we are able to grapple effectively with them, every attempt at strengthening our democratic society will ultimately fail.

The Christian faith has a long-time acquaintance with these spiritual problems. In fact, they form the factual basis for the theological doctrine of human depravity. The Christian faith has learned the hard way that a man must struggle from the very beginning of his life against this grim and forbidding heritage. So far from being stopped by the doctrine of original sin, the Christian faith announces the doctrine of the grace of God! It says in no uncertain terms that these sins can be conquered, conquered by faith in a God of love whose love is strong enough to overcome any evil, One who is near each person.

The individual can submit to God's will so completely that his reason and conscience will be able to curb and control, even though they can never eradicate, the tendency toward greed, pride, and prejudice. Human reason and conscience are, therefore, the gifts of God to man, gifts whereby we can "think his thoughts after him," whereby we seek to order our lives after his will for us. Such gifts remind us that it is never wholly accurate to say, "God has spoken." The truth of the matter is that God not only has spoken, but continues to speak to those who are willing to hear. The fact of God is the bedrock upon which the Christian faith bases its triumphant confidence in man and in the future.

Persons who have made the Christian religion the basis for their faith continue to believe that men are sons of God. But as our own sons can leave home against our will, so we can leave the family of God. We can forsake the meaning of sonship to him. That does not mean that God forsakes us; he will follow us wherever we go, seeking to win us again to the relationship of love. Once we submit mind and will to the will of God as we see it in Jesus Christ, we gain a sense of direction. Slowly we win the strength to move away from that kind of degradation of life which these perennial threats bring to human nature. It is God who enables us to have the strength and the courage so to move.

The Christian answers the question, "Are we capable of democracy?" in this way: "With God's help, yes. We are capable of fashioning a society of the people, by the people, and for the people which shall not perish from the earth. It is possible for us, by means of reason and conscience, under the guidance of God, to live in such a way that we can learn to love each other and to live together as a family, recognizing the fact that another has a claim upon our concern and co-operation, not simply as a citizen, but as a brother in Christ."

III

The Christian witness can help democracy accept and adjust to the tremendous problems of social change. Dr. Toynbee gives as his first reason for the decay and disintegration of civilization "the intractability of institutions." It is a fact, of course, that established institutions are characterized by a blind resistance to change. They become complacent, self-satisfied, and self-perpetuating. They magnify their virtues and minimize their vices. They trumpet their achievements to the heavens, but "mum's the word" about their shortcomings. They seek "good men," "safe men," for positions of leadership, men who can be trusted to give the applecart a gentle ride. They reserve their choicest epithets for anyone who demands a drastic change in affairs. He is an agitator, a troublemaker, a rabble rouser, an anarchist. He will be called a socialist, Communist, or fascist, depending upon which way the international winds happens to be blowing at the moment. Is this "intractability of institutions" as inevitable as it is fatal?

Two facts deserve a hearing as we seek an answer. First, we seem to be afraid of the future. On the whole, we would rather endure the ills we have than fly to others we know not of. Consequently, even those who suffer injustice under the established institution would rather continue under it than risk worse under something else—until, of course, like the peasants in the French Revolution, their agony becomes unendurable. Then the deluge comes.

Second, privileged groups tend to freeze the *status quo* at the point of their maximum privilege. Political machines are excellent examples of privileged groups in politics. They vigorously resist all changes that they cannot turn to their own immediate political advantage. They control elections, by foul means as frequently as fair; they seek to defame rather than answer critics of their policy. Although they know all of the catch words of democracy, its spirit is far from them.

Yet change must and will come—we have no choice in the matter. People will not starve quietly in a world of actual and potential plenty. They will not forever bear patiently indignities and inequities based upon race. They will not endure endlessly domination by another people. Change will come, must come; preferably by evolution, but that failing, by revolution.

The Christian faith has real assistance to offer the democratic ideal at this point. For Christians of all people ought to be prepared to face the fact that changes must come; they ought to be ready to lead in the search for the proper form the change should take. As a matter of fact, a vital Christian faith will inaugurate many fundamental social changes, because it cannot rest content with the social order in which we live.

Jesus felt that all vital religion is a leaven which keeps

working until it "leaveneth the whole lump." Its work is never done. The leaven of the Christian faith is its basic convictions about God, Christ, and the good life. It begins with the reality and centrality of God in life and in the universe. It moves from this to the position that we have our clearest revelation of his will for men in the life and teachings of Jesus Christ. It concludes by emphasizing the possibility of the good life as one in which the God-given rights of personal dignity, worth, and freedom develop in terms of social privilege and responsibility.

Ideas like these have brought about some of the most significant developments imaginable. Consider how the lot of the slave, the peasant, and the laboring man in the Greco-Roman world in the second century, for example, was made easier by the leaven of the Christian religion. For whenever one of these persons in the downtrodden classes of that day became a Christian, he immediately ceased to be a slave in spirit; he stepped into a fellowship which accepted him as a brother in Christ and an equal before God. This was a status no slave, workingman, or peasant in the Greco-Roman world had ever dreamed possible. The Christian witness, like light in darkness, proclaimed that he was that sort of person, entitled to live in that sort of fellowship. Nor was it a verbal reward. When he became a member of that warm fellowship, it easily meant more than any other relationship. It opened his days with a meeting for song and prayer; it closed with a common meal out of which the communion service grew. It surrounded his days with a kind of spiritual ministration, making sacraments of them. It said to the underprivileged, the dispossessed man of the ancient world, "You have an immortal soul worth more than your body will ever be worth. See to it that your immortal soul is safely kept in God's control. You have nothing to fear from man in this life."

That approach obviously would not and did not result in a head-on assault on the institution of slavery. But the end of slavery was assured when the Christian religion planted the ideal of brotherhood in every "handbook of Christian ethics." For slavery and brotherhood have nothing, finally, in common; nor have serfdom and brotherhood. There is no place in the Christian conception of brotherhood for the exploitation of human beings, whether individuals or races. There is no way we can so pervert the Christian ethic as to sanction the kinds of discrimination which somehow have been clung to jealously by men and women, even in the name of Christ, through years and centuries. When the seeds of brotherhood are sown in a social order, they are perennials that will keep right on pushing up the plants of justice and equity until underprivilege and dispossession cease to be characteristics of that society.

As long as we keep on being witnesses to the faith that all men are sons of God and equal in the sight of God, we shall be making progress toward changing the social institutions of our day. It may be that the only progress we are able to discern in any given age is this: Our institutions will be brought under the judgment of that insight. That is a prerequisite of process; for an institution must be seen to be failing, to be inadequate, before men will try to change it fundamentally.

Looking over Christian history, then, we ought to be prepared to face the plain fact that changes must come. They have come and they will continue to come in our social order, for the Christian religion cannot be content with the social order in which we live. It probes our way of life with a keen, razor-edged ethic that brings under the judgment of God's will and love not only our own personal lives and sins but also our institutions—family, school, church, government, economic order. Under the heading of that ethic one basic question is raised: How shall the needed changes be brought about? All that we are or hope to be, all that we hold dear, all that we have found good must continue to grow "in the grace of God unto perfection."

IV

In still another way the Christian witness pours courage into the flagging democratic ideal in our time. It helps cherish and cultivate many values that are as essential to democracy as to religion. Religion and democracy must of necessity hinder or help each other because they work on the same person at the same time. There is this difference between them, however; they work on different levels of that person's thought and life. Their vital relationship might be pictured this way: Their efforts parallel each other in principle on almost all issues. But they form a horizontal rather than vertical parallel in the life of any given person. Religion is the lower line of the parallel, dealing with the universal implications of human life and faith. Democracy is the upper line, dealing with the responsibilities of the person to the particular segment of human life and society of which he is a part.

If religion is successful as it works at the lower level, democracy is strengthened. If democracy is successful as it works at the upper level, inevitably the significance of religion in human life is enormously enlarged. If democracy fails at the upper level, religion is weakened and hindered (but does not necessarily fail), though if religion fails at the lower level, democracy necessarily fails. That is why it is at least a half-truth to say that "democracy and religion stand or fall together." The meaning of this co-operation between the upper and lower levels of democracy and religion in personal life will be clarified if we see their efforts in operation in concrete cases.

1. *Both democracy and the Christian faith find their surest guarantee for the future in their confidence in man.*

Democracy says: "All men are created equal." That is *almost* a Christian answer. It would be entirely so if it read, "All men are created equal and brothers one of another." We are still waiting for the Christian answer to find its way as leaven through the law, institutions, and practices of this land.

Ethical religion is duty bound to challenge the right of some to have more than they need while others have less than they need of the necessities of life. For democracy, this kind of injustice and inequity is a misreading of the constitutional effort to guarantee to all men the right to life, liberty, and the pursuit of happiness. For religion, it is a perversion of God's providence as we see it in the abundance of nature which man does not create, but appropriates for the nourishment of his own life. For one man to take more than he needs while another is unable to get as much as he needs is a misunderstanding of the worth and responsibility with which God has endowed every man. Christian ethics demands a rebuilding, not a redecoration, of society at this point. And we have no right to claim exemption from that kind of radical reconstruction which must come about as we seek a more Christian social order. The task is clearly a part of the Christian witness; our work is cut out for us. We must do everything in our power to see to it that the Christian gospel of the worth of the individual and the equality of all men in the sight of God becomes a molding force in our churches and throughout the entire social order.

2. *Both democracy and the Christian faith agree that the individual must be kept conscious of the larger whole of which he is a part.*

Democracy visualizes the larger whole in terms of "general welfare" and "majority rule." Whenever we move into an election year we hear much of these conceptions. They underlie our constitutional practices, remind us that we are parts of the larger whole and should conduct ourselves accordingly. The Christian faith, working at the deeper level, likewise seeks to keep us conscious of a larger whole. But it does not limit its concern to the citizens of this or any other nation. It is interested in the welfare of all men, in the brotherhood of man. Whereas democracy speaks of the will of the majority, Christian faith speaks of the will of God. The Christian faith talks in terms of the unity of all men everywhere in God, and seeks to awaken in the individual a keen consciousness of his relationship to and interdependence with the larger whole.

Neither democracy nor religion can tolerate any form of self-sufficient individualism in which the individual defines himself in opposition to the welfare of the larger whole. "Rugged individualism," as such, may have been possible in the days of the pioneer era of this country; it may still be possible for a Robinson Crusoe on an island, but its number has long since been called in human history. Now we must bend our best efforts toward finding the meaning of freedom within community. Religion's long experience—and tragic as well—in this area enables it to be of great service to democracy. For religion has been trying for many centuries to persuade men that they must define their own welfare and freedom in terms of the welfare and freedom of all men everywhere. So long as one man is in chains anywhere on the face of the earth, we must deal with the fact of slavery; so long as one man is hungry somewhere, we must seek to conquer the fact of hunger. A fair way to describe the relationship is to say that what democracy seeks for the life of a given people, religion seeks for mankind.

3. Democracy and the Christian faith alike seek to prepare a man to bear responsibility.

Democracy does this in a thoroughgoing manner. It sets before every man the choice of a profession, of his life companion, of the kind of home he wants to have, of who shall be his leaders in civic life, of standards of values by which he will live, of the church in which he will be a member and seek to rear his children.

The Christian faith seeks to train men to the point where they can bear the responsibility of making over-all decisions for their lives. With all its exaltation of the supremacy of the will of God, it in nowise minimizes the importance of personal decision. Turn to the Old Testament strain, "Choose you this day whom ye will serve." (Joshua 24:15.) Or to the New Testament: "If any man will come after me, let him deny himself, and take up his cross daily, and follow me." (Luke 9:23.) These insights illustrate the manner in which every man must choose, and bear the responsibility of that choice. Martin Luther called this fact "the priesthood of all believers." Every man stands before God as a person and seeks to relate himself to the will of God. It is not necessary for him to have an intermediary in the form of a priest through whom he makes his peace with the will of God. Each man must bear full responsibility for his own relationship to that will. A man must answer to God, and to him more than anyone else, for the deepest decisions regarding the life he lives. All of the choices we make must finally square with God's will for us and for all who are affected by our choice—this is the stern admonition of religion.

4. While both democracy and the Christian faith emphasize the freedom of the individual, they are gravely troubled over its meaning.

Mr. Walter Lippmann defines freedom, as we find it in

democracy, in a very emphatic and somewhat negative way:
"Freedom is the right to look any man in the eye and tell
him to go to hell." Religion puts it positively but none the
less dramatically, "Freedom is the right to look any man in
the eye and hail him as brother." Neither religion nor
democracy tolerates castes or inherited ranks. All honor
accorded an individual must be in recognition of his own
worth. We regard freedom as a virtue because it is essential
to social and personal growth. Thus we treasure as fundamental such freedoms as freedom of information, freedom of
criticism, and freedom of creative energies and expressions.
In no other way can we keep a social order or a church
adjusted to the changing needs of an ever changing world.

Freedom takes still another concrete form for both religion
and democracy, one so hotly contested today that it deserves
special mention. I refer to the freedom of a new idea or
institution to win a following at the expense of accepted ideas
and existing institutions. Since the latter framed the conventions and wrote the laws, the former has a hard time of it.
One of the most pertinent examples of this tension is to be
found in the fact that, today, it is accepted religious and legal
doctrine south of the Rio Grande that evangelical churches
(Protestant) shall not be permitted to win adherents from
among those who are nominally related to the Roman Catholic
Church. That kind of prohibition, of course, cuts across the
fundamental meaning of freedom for both democracy and
religion alike. If for some reason we desire to break away
from a given political party or the established church, we
must have the freedom both to do that and to win a following
for what we are doing. This truth was never put more suc-
cinctly than by Abraham Lincoln in a speech on the Mexican
War. He observed that whenever the people of a country
"grow weary of the existing government, they can exercise

their constitutional right of amending it, or their revolutionary right to dismember or overthrow it."

I know of no way to maintain a strong emphasis upon freedom without opening doors that look in a direction that is dangerous in many respects. Even Lincoln's statement portrays this danger. But it is infinitely more dangerous to close those doors than it is to open them, especially in these days when freedom is on trial, when the right of free men to think out their problems and live their lives as seems best to them is being challenged the world around.

Another way to put the matter is to say that freedom is a virtue for both democracy and religion because conscience is a fact in human life and experience. When we speak of conscience, we are not talking about some abstract thing. We are talking about the ability of each individual to face the issues of his day, to take his own stand, and to feel that this is the proper thing to do. Conscience as such is the gift of God. It is the ability to glimpse in a flash of insight our total responsibility for the problem before us. Freedom of conscience, so conceived, is essential to democracy and religion alike. When the Supreme Court rules, as it did with some frequency in "war years," that the freedom of conscience must be subordinated to the will of the majority, thoughtful religionists gird on their spiritual armor and take the field at once. For the right of conscience is more than the possibility of social anarchy, it is the right to live as a human being.

V

The Christian faith, then, makes three indispensable contributions to the survival of democracy. It strives to transform man until he becomes a fit citizen of a social order dedicated to the ideal of brotherhood. It strives to transform a social order until it both deserves and nurtures the life of such citizens. It stands at the side of the democratic ideal, cherishing and cultivating many of the same profound ideals and values. Canon F. R. Barry was speaking to both democracy and religion when he wrote:

> We are back on our ultimate ethical resources. What Democracy needs for its survival is the leadership of spiritual conviction. Only so far as it is reestablished on its true moral and religious basis is there any hope that it can endure and move to the next stage in its development. All that we value most in our tradition is the gift of our ancestral Christianity; all we can hope to contribute to the future is inseparably bound up with it.[2]

The Christian religion stands far beyond the forms of democracy that we now enjoy, and says, "Come up higher." It beckons us, bogged down as we are in the antagonisms, injustices, and other evils of our day, and says, "They must be conquered if you would live. They will not conquer themselves, but you have both the right and the power under God to master them before they destroy you." Mankind in general and this nation in particular, kept consciously under God, can achieve a much higher form of democracy than history has ever known. George Washington saw this when, in his Farewell Address, he urged his fellow countrymen to pay constant and reverent attention to the worship of God. "Can it be," he asked, "that Providence has not connected the permanent felicity of a nation with its virtue?"

Abraham Lincoln saw it when he said, "This nation, under God, shall have a new birth of freedom." Woodrow Wilson saw it in *The Road Away from Revolution* when he said, "The

[2] F. R. Barry, *What Has Christianity to Say?* (New York, Harper & Bros., 1938), page 31. Used by permission.

sum of the whole matter is this, that our civilization cannot survive materially unless it be redeemed spiritually. It can be saved only by becoming permeated with the spirit of Christ and being made free and happy by the practices which spring out of that spirit. Only thus can discontent be driven out and all the shadows lifted from the road ahead."

But each of these great leaders of democracy saw that we as individuals must sense our relationship and responsibility to God before we as a people can hope to fashion an enduring democracy. That is a step which no leader can take for us. But, under God, we can take it for ourselves if we lose not first our faith, then our courage.

10

War and Peace

I

I T IS a grim truism of our time that the problems of peace
and war are the problems of life and death for our civilization—perhaps even for man on this planet. That is why
Christian churches are paying more serious attention to them.
For the last fifty years they have provided the main center
of interest in conferences of churchmen gathered to discuss
the role of the church in the contemporary world.

Churches share this concern with every other responsible
group, as a survey of the reports of any major meeting of
business, industry, labor, education, government, or law will
show. Great as are the special problems in each of these
areas, none looms half so high as the problems of war and
peace.

When the distinguished attorney, Mr. Charles S. Rhyne,
gave the annual presidential address of the American Bar
Association in Los Angeles in 1958, he bypassed the strictly
legal problems that confront his profession and chose as his
theme, "World Peace Through Law."

He began with the simple assertion that the number one
problem of mankind today is how to achieve and maintain
world peace. Admittedly, he felt forced by contemporary

events to suggest radical surgery in our ordinary thought about ourselves and the state of the world. Social, scientific, and political events have conspired to alter in every fundamental way our outlook on today and tomorrow. The usual methods of military force, diplomacy, trade, and negotiation, at best, have produced an armistice, a breathing space, but not peace, or even the likelihood of peace. Mr. Rhyne then advanced a carefully thought out plan for world peace through law that looks far beyond anything yet seriously suggested as an alternative to the "drift toward destruction." He called upon the members of the bar to accept the task of working out the basic concepts of world law and a world court system far more realistic and relevant than anything yet attempted.

This epochal address by Mr. Rhyne deserves careful attention not alone because of its intrinsic merit, but also because it helps us see the situation that responsible people now face. They are being forced either to think for themselves or to let someone else do their thinking for them in this area where the issues of life or death for mankind are now fully, finally, and should we fail, fatally joined.

Even those among us most willing to think about these problems are frankly appalled at the number and complexity of the issues that demand a hearing. We feel as though we need to be three of four different kinds of scientist, diplomat, historian, lawyer, educator, philosopher of religion, and common man—all rolled into one. That kind of knowledge and background is necessary to appreciate the true meaning of the major issues involved in war and peace. No one can be all of these, but we must still think, decide, and act.

As the Christian seeks to find the Christian way of life in this troubled field, there are certain general rules of thought which will help him to a considered judgment.

II

First of all, one who thinks about war and peace has a spiritual obligation to keep fully informed on the major issues involved, and to think realistically about them. Simply to sketch the ones that occupy the center of the stage in the United Nations is a sobering experience.

Hunger is and always has been the greatest enemy to peace known to man. Two-thirds of the people now alive are undernourished and suffer the diseases that prey on the hungry. They suffer the additional awareness that other peoples are not undernourished, and further that they themselves need not be. Famine, want, and hunger are no longer accepted as inevitable, as plagues to be endured as from God or fate. They are remediable ills, and the means with which to remedy them are available.

The day of the very rich and the very poor is drawing to a welcome close from one end of this earth to the other. Call it by whatever name we will, and in whatever spirit we choose, the fact is undeniable. Whether by taxes, which practically confiscate wealth for the individual, or by foreign aid programs, which share the wealth of the favored nations with the underdeveloped areas of the world, the process of closing the chasms in the human family is now under way on a world-wide scale. And strangely, but humanly enough, the pressure to close the gap comes from both sides of the chasm. The need of the less favored pushes from one side, and the conscience of the more favored pushes from the other.

Living as we do in one of the most favored situations ever known to man, we are unable, and few have the desire any more to try, to build walls between ourselves and the rest of the world. Let desperate need arise, whether in Hungary, Africa, or Tibet, and we expect and want to help meet it as best we can. If India needs a gigantic hydroelectric program for irrigation, conservation, and power in order to lift her standard of living, we ought to help, and we will. The conscience of many Americans was deeply offended in 1957 when our government withdrew aid from the Aswan Dam in Egypt, thus confessing that our aid is predicated not on the needs of people but on our own military necessity.

Problems like these which arise from hunger and malnutrition in large areas of the world are ours to accept for study, understanding, and aid. This we must do, if we are to think realistically about the Christian way of life in relation to problems of war and peace.

We have a spiritual obligation to be informed and to think realistically about another great fact. There is great significance in the world-wide surge toward new freedom, or at least toward new forms of life which promise freedom to at least half of the people on earth. The social, economic, and political revolutions which began in 1900 in China have produced a slow but definite chain reaction everywhere. The efforts either to exploit or to contain them have kept Asia in turmoil for nearly half a century. And the whole world has been involved in them from the very beginning. Mistakes aplenty in foreign policy and deed are plain to hindsight; but the only really irremediable mistake open to us now is to refuse to recognize the fast, unstoppable surge to new social, political, and economic forms of life all over the world.

Our obvious alarm over this surge would be easier to understand if we in the United States had been standing still since 1619, when the first colonists landed—or even since 1900! As we well know, ours has been and continues to be what can only be called a "dynamic economy"; it has never stood still. And we have not found any way even to slow down the rate of change in it. We have moved from the economy of a colony on the frontier to a most complex industrialized nation. Our population has moved from a society numbered in thousands to 180 million, from one divided into classes to as near a "class-less" society as man has seen. We have moved from weakness to strength, from nationalism to internationalism, from complete absorption in our own affairs to an awareness of and concern for the affairs of the rest of the world.

What has happened here is happening everywhere—rapid, epoch-making changes are under way. One who seeks to bear the Christian witness in such a time will need to be informed and will want to have both an understanding mind and a sympathetic heart. The problems that have surged into existence with these changes belong to the problems of war and peace in our time.

So also with the problem of disarmament. The United States and every other major country seems to be impaled on the horns of a dilemma on this matter.

On the one hand, we are rearming with desperate speed; on the other, we say we want to disarm quickly if any plan can be agreed upon. The sheer lunacy of flirting with a nuclear war is obvious to all, but we tell ourselves that only the strong can hope to survive. We are deeply disturbed by conflicting scientific reports over the danger to life through continued nuclear testing; yet we argue that we must keep the program going until there is agreement on how best to stop it.

Most of us could do with much more information on these matters than we now have. It is available, if we are willing to take the time to follow through on it. Unless we do so, we shall be voting blind on men and policies that deal with life or death for all.

If we are to think realistically about war and peace, we

must cultivate a new sense of honesty in the use of ideas like "limited war," or, as the Pentagon puts it, "brush-fire war."

This is easily one of the most dangerously vague concepts in current usage. It deliberately obscures one of the most ominous new facts we should be facing in all honesty.

No one is or can be sure that a limited war is any longer possible. There is no assurance that wars will spread slowly any more; there is every reason to believe they will explode with full violence almost at once. The Korean War may well have been the last one that can be limited in any sense at all. All major powers were on hand in force in the Near Eastern crisis over Quemoy in the summer of 1958; the United States and Russia were there hurling threats of immediate war if either made a move.

Even to use the concept "limited war" gives an illusion of security from all-out nuclear war. We justify our vast foot-soldier program, our retention of the Selective Service program, and the steady expansion of military influence in government by saying that they will enable us to go anywhere on earth and put out a "brush-fire war."

In order to think realistically on such matters we need to keep in mind the absolute nature of the choice before us as we consider the problems of war and peace. (1) We are not choosing between communism and democracy; the choice is between life and death for all men on this planet. (2) We dare not even momentarily be content with the existence of a truce, a cold war, a breathing space; we must have peace and we must keep peace, or we shall all perish.

III

Christians in the United States have a spiritual obligation to be informed on the basic issues involved in war and

peace. Moreover, we need to know that Christians all over
the world are similarly concerned with these issues. The rapid
growth of the ecumenical movement, drawing churches together in an unprecedented way, has made it possible for us
to know that churchmen in Asia, Africa, and all other parts
of the world are thinking about common problems.

The Second Assembly of the World Council of Churches,
meeting in Evanston in 1954, spent much of its time trying
to fashion the Christian witness on the problems of war and
peace. It was a sobering thing to have conscientious Christians
from thirty different countries—some behind the iron cur-
tain—meet and seek a Christian approach to these matters.

The report of the Evanston Assembly reveals several important points of agreement among them.

To begin with, the Christian church is thoroughly dis-
illusioned about war: "Deeply and persistently man longs for
peace. He no longer finds any glamour in war; he has tasted
the fruit of its insanity and found it bitter and poisonous. His
ideals are mocked, his liberty curtailed, his possessions de-
stroyed, and his future undermined by total war even as its
high-sounding goals have eluded his grasp. He is sick of it,
and wants to be at peace!" [1]

The idealistic garb that frequently masks war is ripped off
in two cryptic sentences: "Lofty objectives so often invented
to justify war cannot conceal the truth that its violence and
destruction are inherently evil. Therefore Christians, in their
respective countries, must not lend themselves to, but expose,
this deceit." [2]

The armaments race was denounced for the gigantic lie it
is. It may promise peace, but it is a matter of historical record

[1] W. A. Visser 't Hooft (ed.), *The Evanston Report* (New York, Harper &
Bros., 1955), pages 131-2. Used by permission.

[2] *Ibid.*, page 132. Used by permission.

that every armaments race in history has promised peace, yet
ended in a major war.

Pacifist and nonpacifist alike in the World Council agreed
on this characterization of war, however much they continued
to disagree on other issues. The Evanston Report said everything about war that a confirmed pacifist might wish the
church to say, without trespassing in the sacred area of
conscience. There every man must decide for himself what
he will do in case of conflict. But it did warn all who go to
war, whether for conscience' sake or not, that war will betray
every hope and give the lie to every sacrifice made in it.
Which is a way of saying, "Go to war if you feel you must;
but go with the clear realization that your sacrifices will be
wasted, your idealism will be mocked, and the waging of the
war will bring to an end the 'great experiment' called
humanity."

There was further agreement that "It is not enough for
the churches to proclaim that war is evil. They must study
afresh the Christian approaches to peace, . . . they must seek
out, analyze, and help to remove the psychological and social,
and political and economic causes of war. Without forsaking
their conviction that all weapons of war are evil, the churches
should press for restraints on their use. Christians in all lands
must plead with their government to be patient and persistent
in their search for means to limit weapons and advance disarmament." [3]

The realism with which the Christian witness views the
dangers of disarmament and looks beyond them toward a day
when they will not be needed is plainly stated in these words:
"An international order of truth and peace would require:
(1) under effective international inspection and control and
in such a way that no state would have cause to fear that its

[3] *Ibid.*, page 133. Used by permission.

security was endangered, the elimination and prohibition of atomic, hydrogen and all other weapons of mass destruction, as well as the reduction of all armaments to a minimum; (2) the development and acceptance of methods for peaceful change to rectify existing injustices." [4]

The despair that grips men when they think of the problems of war and peace today is one of the most serious facts to be reckoned with. Actually, it has grown to such proportions that effective thought on it is almost paralyzed. Hypnotized, we wait for the finishing blow. Who will strike it, where it will fall, what the reaction will be—these things seem to be unimportant to us. That is because when it falls, it falls on all. And the complete and overpowering destruction that it will bring is almost beyond our power to imagine.

We would do well to be deeply aware of the despair which chills our spirits today, but we must reject it as being both unwarranted and unchristian. We cannot simply wait around for the grand finale to the human enterprise. We are asked to ". . . bring the transforming power of Jesus Christ to bear upon the hearts of men. Christians must pray more fervently for peace, repent more earnestly of their individual and collective failures to further world order, and strive more urgently to establish world contacts for reconciliation, fellowship and love." [5] The one great hope for the future lies in persons with this kind of Christian zeal.

The World Council asks that our witness fashion itself on certain basic facts. (1) Peace requires a foundation of moral principles rooted in the love of God as we see it in Jesus Christ. (2) Peace requires a system of justice which articulates and defends human rights, not only as we understand them but as our understanding will grow with our experience.

[4] *Ibid.*, page 133. Used by permission.

[5] *Ibid.*, page 132. Used by permission.

V

So far as the first recommendation is concerned—peace requires a foundation of moral principles—the World Council says that the shape of things to come will be determined for good, if men are willing to think and act in the light of these convictions.

1. All power carries responsibility and all nations are trustees of power which should be used for the common good.

2. All nations are subject to moral law, and should strive to abide by the accepted principles of international law, to develop this law, and to enforce it through common actions.

3. All nations should honour their pledged word and international agreements into which they have entered.

4. No nation in an international dispute has the right to be sole judge in its own cause or to resort to war to advance its policies, but should seek to settle disputes by direct negotiation or by submitting them to conciliation, arbitration or judicial settlement.

5. All nations have a moral obligation to ensure universal security and to this end should support measures designed to deny victory to a declared aggressor.

6. All nations should recognize and safeguard the inherent dignity, worth and essential rights of the human person, without distinction as to race, sex, language or religion.

7. Each nation should recognize the rights of every other nation, which observes such standards, to live by and proclaim its own political and social beliefs, provided that it does not seek by coercion, threat, infiltration or deception to impose these on other nations.

8. All nations should recognize an obligation to

share their scientific and technical skills with peoples in less developed regions, and to help the victims of disaster in other lands.

9. All nations should strive to develop cordial relations with their neighbours, encourage friendly cultural and commercial dealings, and join in creative international efforts for human welfare.[6]

Nor were these resolutions left hanging in the air. *The Evanston Report* goes on to say that in addition to this broad moral foundation, peace requires a system of justice which will articulate and defend human rights.

One firm impression comes from participating in assemblies of churchmen from all over the world who are trying to think together about the meaning of the Christian way of life in the problems of war and peace: We are moving away from the idea of separate and sovereign states toward some sort of a more powerful United Nations or form of world federation. The conviction is everywhere present that *nationalism* or the determination to set one's country apart from, if not over against other countries, is the "villain of the peace" of our time. The delegates from Asia and Africa repeatedly warned that nationalism is their greatest enemy now. Representatives from Europe and the United States could assure them from their own unfinished experience that this estimate is undoubtedly correct.

Every major conference of churchmen since the founding of the United Nations has endorsed the principle and the institution of the United Nations with special emphasis upon the Universal Declaration of Human Rights. Few would claim that these instruments are perfect or fully satisfactory as they are, but they are the best we have, and they can be improved. Christians are called upon to take them for what

[6] *Ibid.*, page 142. Used by permission.

they are—our one chance, perhaps our last one, to move away from world anarchy toward an international system of justice and understanding.

Of course this movement involves the loss of some precious freedom of action on the part of separate nations. How could it be otherwise? Why should we be surprised about it or balk at it? As well expect us to have a United States without federal law and federal government, as the United Nations without some growth of international authority, law, and power at the center. As well try to make a durable, creative marriage union out of two individuals who are more jealously set on preserving their individualities than on developing a new mutuality. A marriage without mutuality is a farce and a failure; equally, a system of world order without an actual growth of mutuality through the surrender of some of the freedoms and rights of national states is certain to fail. And, lest we forget, we cannot afford to fail at this now.

How long will it take to develop real confidence in a foundation of moral principles and in an international system of justice? How long to teach our stubborn spirits to accept the judgment of others, to learn to "live peaceably with all"? Who but God can say? But it is enough for us to know that that is our task, that it begins here and now, and that our Christian comrades—indeed, those from other religions as well—are working at it all over the world.

Those who accuse the Christian church of being an international organization do not thereby criticize it; they describe and compliment it. That is what it is in intention, and what it will increasingly become in actual fact. And, God willing, working through people like us and churches like ours, it will lead the nations of the world toward a truly international order which in God's good time will actually become the human family where we will "live peaceably with all."

11

Ecumenical Relations

I

THE MOST serious problem the Christian witness faces today is not opposition from atheist ideologies and rival religions; it is disunity among the churches. This disunity ranges all of the way from simple lack of communication across denominational lines to outright and intemperate attacks upon the theological claims and organizational structures of each other. Fortunately, there is less of the latter than of the former. Differences which half a century ago had the churches in the United States arrayed against each other in varying degrees of violence are now subsiding into a state of toleration and implicit acceptance of the right of each other to live. Fortunately this is proceeding rapidly—and for a very clear reason.

Christians are shamed by and ashamed of disunity. The bland explanation of differences which says that "we are all going toward the same place even though we are traveling different roads" simply does not meet the point of the sin of disunion. There is something incontestably sinful in the spectacle of a half a dozen small churches in a town of moderate size disagreeing with each other, raiding each other's membership, and vying with each other in the rush to per-

suade newcomers that they "ought to come to our church."
It is difficult to believe in the fundamental unity of institutions that conduct themselves in this manner.

Back of such local strife lie the larger areas of conflict
between and among the major churches and traditions of
Christendom: Roman Catholic, Orthodox, Lutheran, Re-
formed, and Free Church, to mention the larger ones. None
of these divisions is new; all have been in existence for
hundreds of years. And the sad tale of separation continues.

In the mission field new churches are coming into existence,
geared to the needs of the people of the various countries:
India, Japan, Africa, and China. Not only are the various
churches in these countries separating themselves from their
parent churches, but they are also running into difficulties
with each other. They may differ over ritual, or beliefs, or
organizations—but out of these differences comes growing
disunity because they fail to exemplify the Christian way of
life.

Yet, ironically, Christians talk about, pray for, and say they
believe in unity. Call it the witness of the Holy Spirit through
our unity in Christ, or "the conscience of the Christian
fellowship," or by any other name; but this protest against
disunity is one of the most significant new facts in Christendom today. The determination to re-examine differences and
to do so in the spirit of Christian fellowship is a well-defined
trend in church thought and life.

There is general agreement among Christians that disunion
is the scandal, sin, and shame of the Christian Church. While
agreement on what ought to be done about it is still lacking,
there is no disagreement on the need to do something. The
Christian churches are highly dissatisfied with division, and
they have begun to do something about it in concrete ways,
and propose to do much more. The major church traditions—

outside Roman Catholicism—have begun to draw together in a serious and sustained fashion in what is known as the "ecumenical movement."

The late Bishop of Chichester, G. K. A. Bell, displayed the British genius for understatement when he said of the word "ecumenical" that it is "an unusual word." Dr. W. A. Visser 't Hooft, general secretary of the World Council of Churches, has made a brief but careful study of the history and usage of the word which will help us to understand its importance.

The Greek word from which it comes occurs fifteen times in the New Testament and means either "the whole inhabited world" or "the Roman Empire." In Christian usage, ecumenical came to mean both "the whole church" and anything regarded as valid throughout the church. Today it has taken on three new meanings: (1) the world-wide missionary outreach of the churches; (2) the growth toward and achievement of actual unity between and among churches; (3) the consciousness of and desire for Christian unity.

In 1937 the Oxford Conference gave "ecumenical" the meaning it carries in the thought of most churchmen today: "The term ecumenical refers to the expression within history of the given unity of the Church. The thought and action of the Church are ecumenical, in so far as they attempt to realize the *Una Sancta,* the fellowship of Christians, who acknowledge the one Lord."[1] The thought in this is clear: God has given the separate Christian churches and traditions a unity in Christ which they must acknowledge and seek to bring to full realization in their common life and witness.

There is an awareness (1) of a divinely given spiritual unity which has become obscured by our divisions, and (2) of the Christian compulsion to recover a visible witness to

[1] Quoted in *A History of the Ecumenical Movement,* Ruth Rouse and S. C. Neill (ed.), (Philadelphia, The Westminster Press, 1954), page 740.

this unity in the life of the churches. This can be found in all major Christian traditions.

II

While the ecumenical movement is broader than the World Council of Churches, it finds its most striking expression in the development of that movement. Space does not permit a detailed description of the entire process by which the World Council has come into existence. At different times and for different reasons, essentially the same vision of the needed unity of the church came to Bishop Charles Brent, Anglican missionary bishop to the Philippine Islands, Archbishop Nathan Soderblom of Sweden, and John R. Mott, a Methodist layman from this country. Each in his own way began to interest others and work toward conferences in which scattered churches would be drawn together for the purpose of discussing their differences. Undismayed by two world wars and chronic denominational suspicions, these men and others persisted in their task. Then came that great day in Amsterdam in August of 1948 when the Archbishop of Canterbury, in opening the First General Assembly of the World Council of Churches, declared that the World Council of Churches was both in being and in session. The assembly then proclaimed this conviction to the world:

> Christ has made us His own, and He is not divided. In seeking Him we find one another. Here at Amsterdam we have committed ourselves afresh to Him, and have covenanted with one another in constituting this World Council of Churches. We intend to stay together.[2]

[2] *Man's Disorder and God's Design*, The Amsterdam Assembly Series. (New York, Harper & Bros., 1949). Used by permission.

Six years later the ecumenical movement drove its roots still more deeply into the consciousness of the life of the Christian world, when, in the Second Assembly in Evanston, it said:

> Six years ago our churches entered into a covenant to form this Council, and affirmed their intention to stay together. We thank God for His blessing on our work and fellowship during these six years. We enter now upon a second stage. To stay together is not enough. We must go forward. As we learn more of our unity in Christ, it becomes the more intolerable that we should be divided.[3]

It is clear to anyone who studies the documents that the World Council of Churches is not and does not intend to be a "super-church." It is a *council of churches* that is working to join in "a fellowship of conversation, mutual enrichment, common witness, and common action."[4] What may emerge "in the end" no one can say, but as of now the World Council of Churches is comprised of and open to churches who understand that the council is "a fellowship of churches which accepts our Lord Jesus Christ as God and Saviour."

More than one hundred and seventy churches are in the World Council and bring within its areas of influence over two hundred million confessing Christians. And the end of its development is not yet!

III

One of the most challenging results of the ecumenical efforts to date has been a listing of the points on which we are

[3] W. A. Visser 't Hooft (ed.), *The Evanston Report* (New York, Harper & Bros., 1955), page 2. Used by permission.

[4] W. A. Visser 't Hooft, *The Meaning of Ecumenical* (London, S.C.M. Press, 1954).

actually united. While much work remains to be done in interpreting them, we see even in our present points of agreement the coming unity of Christian churches in and through the Christian witness.

We are united in Jesus Christ. By this, the ecumenical movement means that Christians are united through their own personal experience of finding God in Jesus Christ. He is the one through whom all find deliverance from sin and death. All hail him "Lord and Saviour." Deeper, then, than the differences among the churches in the World Council is this consciousness of sharing in the saving experience of finding God in Jesus Christ.

Even though expressions of this experience will vary from person to person and church to church, there is a growing acceptance among the churches of the genuineness of the religious experience of each other. Even though we may continue to differ on forms of church polity and creedal expression, we accept each other as being "good Christians." Our unity in Jesus Christ is the area of agreement within our disagreements.

Another powerful force behind the ecumenical movement is the discovery that all churches accept the New Testament emphasis upon our unity in Christ. The New Testament reveals the unifying work of Christ among the Christians of that early day. There is the famous passage in the Gospel of John which begins, "I am the vine, ye are the branches." There is Paul's well-known metaphor of Christ as the head and his disciples as members of one body. Perhaps the most famous of all is Paul's discovery that Christ breaks down all partitions that separate men: "There is neither Jew nor Greek, there is neither slave nor free, there is neither male nor female; for you are all one in Christ Jesus." (Galatians 3:28, Revised Standard Version.)

A third discovery in ecumenical experience is that the longer we stay together and the more sincerely we try to understand each other, the more certain we are that we belong in close communion with each other.

The World Council of Churches suggests a series of "musts" to all Christians who are interested in furthering the spirit of communion in and among the churches:

1. We must keep our divisions under the judgment of our unity. Admittedly, it is hard to do this, but the effort must be made to listen to "our one Lord" speaking to us, and the effort must be made at precisely those points where it is hardest, namely, when we want to insist upon the validity of our points in division.

2. "We must consider frankly the influence of social and cultural differences upon the matters of faith and order which cause divisions, and also perceive how the events and developments of current history make disunity a most urgent question.

3. "We must speak the truth in love with one another and practice that love towards those with whom we disagree. . . .

4. "We must seek to acknowledge beyond the bounds of our own church each ministry that preaches the gospel of reconciliation as a means whereby Christ performs His saving deeds. . . .

5. "We must bear witness together to the gospel of Him who has already overcome our sins and divisions and who graciously uses sinners as His servants. Our divided witness is a necessarily defective witness, indeed a scandal in the face of the non-Christian world. We have scarcely begun to work out the essential connection between 'mission' and 'unity.' Our Lord's own prayer . . . must become our own, not only on our lips but in our lives."

6. We must pray for unity. "We cannot expect God to give us unity unless we prepare ourselves to

receive His gift by costly and purifying prayer. To
pray *together* is to be drawn together." [5]

IV

The prayers for unity and the efforts of a generation of
dedicated churchmen toward that end have begun to bear
tangible fruit in the witness of the Church in our time. Slowly but surely the separate churches of Christendom are beginning to take account of the World Council of Churches
as an indispensable instrument in the development of unity
in the Christian witness. The World Council now seeks to
pursue its ecumenical aim through the activities of a well-
defined organization with three divisions.

The division of studies seeks to "co-ordinate all work of a
study nature." Study conferences dealing with many points
have already been held and others are in prospect. The different traditions in Christendom are becoming acutely aware
of the actual nature of their differences. It is a staggering
and creative shock when representatives of the "free
churches" and representatives of the Orthodox tradition
begin to discuss "the authority of the church," or "the Second
Coming," or "apostolic succession." While the studies of the
World Council, to date, have not resolved these differences,
they have placed them within the area of continuing studies
and conferences. If ever they are to be resolved, it will be in
this setting.

The division of ecumenical action seeks to help churches
make their membership in the World Council "a practical,
living reality." Through a whole series of departments—
beamed toward youth, men and women, the laity, and leaders

[5] W. A. Visser 't Hooft, *The Evanston Report* (New York, Harper & Bros.,
1955), pages 90-91. Used by permission.

in ecumenical studies—this division pursues its objectives.

Through the division of interchurch aid and service to refugees, the World Council enables its member churches to be anywhere on earth with tangible relief when expulsion or war separate people from their homeland.

The World Council has a Commission of the Churches on International Affairs. Thus churches are represented when international affairs are discussed. They are also kept informed about international conferences which deal with the grave issues of our time.

V

The move toward ecumenical action proceeds on still another level, namely, that of community, state, and national councils of churches. All three are found in the United States and provide our firmest basis for co-operation. They deserve much wider support than they usually receive from denominations and local churches. Yet with even the limited resources at their disposal, the rapid growth of the local and state councils is one of outstanding developments in Protestantism in America today. With wholehearted support by member churches, they can become a very significant expression of unity on the local level.

Interestingly, there is a drawing together of churches in various general regions of the world—North America, Europe, Latin America, Africa, and Asia. A special report published by the *Ecumenical Press Service* on January 16, 1959, carries the simple statement, "For the first time on record an overwhelming majority of the Protestant and Orthodox Churches of Europe have decided to establish methods of continuing co-operation." This was done at what was called the European Church Conference held in Nyborg,

Denmark, January 6-9, 1959. Representatives came from churches in all countries including Russia and Hungary. The First Assembly of the East Asia Christian Conference, with representatives from forty-eight churches and councils in fourteen countries, met in May of 1959 in Kuala Lumpur, Malaya. Similar conferences have been held in Africa and Latin America, with others to follow in all these areas. In this movement we witness a significant growth toward unity in every quarter of Christendom.

Still another form taken by the growth toward unity is the actual merger of existing churches—a process which is going on apace all over the world. Dean J. Robert Nelson gave the Oberlin Conference this startling summary:

> A . . . fascinating task we have is to trace the astonishing progress in the direction of intercommunion and church union. The plain facts contradict all notions that the urge for unity has spent its force. Are you Lutheran, Anglican, Baptist, Presbyterian-Reformed, Disciple, Methodist, Quaker, Mennonite, Moravian, or already partly United? Are you from Canada, the United States, Mexico, Jamaica, Uruguay or Argentina; from Great Britain, Holland, Germany, Poland, Italy or Spain; from Ghana, Nigeria, Kenya, Northern Rhodesia, South Africa, or Madagascar; from Pakistan, India, Ceylon, Indonesia, Japan, Australia or New Zealand? Then you may know that in at least one of these countries there are churches of your own confessional family which are now engaged in serious official negotiations which lead towards a relationship of intercommunion or even organic merger. Church history provides no record of times even comparable to this one.

It is significant that every denomination now has a commission, committee or board on "church union." The Methodist Church has such a commission elected by the General Conference and composed of representatives from the episcopacy and each jurisdiction. It is currently engaged in conversations with at least two major churches of this country. Whether much, little, or nothing will come of them remains to be seen—but the *official* effort is now being made.

Who can doubt that this thrust toward unity will bring greater strength and meaning to the Christian witness in our time? A divided church cannot help unite a divided world. Yet we face a future in which disunion means annihilation. A. N. Whitehead once observed that all centuries are dangerous, then added, "It is the business of the future to be dangerous." Most people will agree that our future is dangerous enough to frighten the most adventurous of us—unless we see some roadway of hope. The Church is not called upon simply to see this roadway; she must be it. And to do this the Church must actually achieve a greater degree of community and unity in thought and life than now exists. The Church's effectiveness as an agent toward unity among men will be determined primarily by the effectiveness of unity among all the churches.

The positive reason for pursuing the goal of unity can be put very simply: It is an essential part of the gospel that we find in the life and teachings of our Master. When we lose it—if we lose it—we lose all. Keep it, and what Christopher Dawson called "the seed of unity, the principle of spiritual order" will not only be preserved, but will come to fruition in our world through the life and thought of the church. Churches are clear on this—and we are trying to be loyal to it in all we do: Whatever oneness we now have is not of our own making; it is the gift of God in Christ. Of ourselves, we would have shattered the church in spirit and in form long ago, but, by the mercy of God, the spiritual unity of the church is beyond our reach. It is indestructible; it is in Jesus Christ; "he is the vine, we are the branches." We are discovering what we should always have known; the more we center our thoughts, our life, our practices in him, the closer we come together as colleagues and brothers.

In 1938 representatives of the younger churches (as the churches in the mission fields are called)

> . . . one and all gave expressions to the passionate longing that exists in all countries for visible union of the churches. They are aware of the fact of spiritual unity; they record with great thankfulness all the signs of co-operation and understanding that are increasingly seen in various directions, but they realize that this is not enough. Visible and organic union must be our goal.[6]

This is the authentic tradition of the mission field where, of necessity, they pay more attention to the New Testament than to the Reformation. In a real and vibrant way, they center their thought and their life in Jesus Christ, and consequently they find a unity that is not now found among their parent churches. It is altogether probable that we shall live to see the time when the missionary churches will send missionaries to parent churches to help them learn to live together in peace and understanding and to find a greater degree of community with each other. If this should come to pass, it will be another example of how "a little child shall lead them."

VI

Unity, therefore, is primarily a matter of living in Christ and only secondarily a matter of living in communion with

[6] *The Life of the Church,* "The Madras Series," IV, page 377. Used by permission of the International Missionary Council.

each other. Only as we respond affirmatively and in faith to his claim on us will we be able to sense the sin and shame of our separation from others who likewise respond to his claim. Only as we rediscover each other as Christians and move toward the Center can we hope to move closer to each other as Christians. Growth toward unity therefore is not primarily a matter of refinement of social strategy and techniques; it is a growth in grace and love through Jesus Christ. This faith nurtures the growth toward unity among us; it also makes that growth urgent and inevitable.